THE GLOBAL ECONOMIC
CRISIS

ASEAN Studies Centre
Institute of Southeast Asian Studies

Report No. 10

THE GLOBAL ECONOMIC CRISIS
Implications for ASEAN

LSEAS

INSTITUTE OF SOUTHEAST ASIAN STUDIES

Singapore

First published in Singapore in 2010 by
ISEAS Publishing
Institute of Southeast Asian Studies
30 Heng Mui Keng Terrace
Pasir Panjang
Singapore 119614
E-mail: publish@iseas.edu.sg
Website: bookshop.iseas.edu.sg

The responsibility for facts and opinions in this publication rests exclusively with the contributors and their interpretations do not necessarily reflect the views or the policy of the publisher or its supporters.

ISEAS Library Cataloguing-in-Publication Data

The global economic crisis : implications for ASEAN.
(Report / ASEAN Studies Centre ; no. 10).
  1. ASEAN.
  2. Financial crises—Economic aspects—Southeast Asia—Congresses.
  3. Financial crises—Social aspects—Southeast Asia—Congresses.
  4. Southeast Asia—Economic integration—Congresses.
  I. Institute of Southeast Asian Studies. ASEAN Studies Centre.
  II. ASEAN Roundtable (2009 : Singapore)
  III. Series.
JZ5333.5 A9A85 no. 10   2010

ISBN 978-981-4279-41-3 (soft cover)
ISBN 978-981-4279-42-0 (E-book PDF)

Typeset by Superskill Graphics Pte Ltd
Printed in Singapore by Seng Lee Press Pte Ltd

CONTENTS

INTRODUCTION

On 18 June 2009, the ASEAN Studies Centre of the Institute of Southeast Asian Studies and the Konrad Adenauer Stiftung organized the ASEAN Roundtable 2009 with the theme "The Global Economic Crisis: Implications for ASEAN". The brainstorming session gathered experts from the region to discuss the impact of the current economic crisis on ASEAN member countries and its community-building process. It did this through the lens of regional security, the social impact and the economy and finance. The roundtable had Mr Arin Jira, Chairman of the ASEAN Business Advisory Council, as the distinguished luncheon speaker.

The roundtable concluded that the crisis had a significant impact on the region, and ASEAN needed to have a better coordinated approach if it was to weather the storm. The region had taken into account the fact that the developed countries like the United States and the European Union would take a longer time to come out of the crisis. Hence, while export-led growth policies had served the region well in the past, governments now had to adopt policies that were oriented more to the domestic or regional markets. Another conclusion of the roundtable had to do with the notion of "security". The current economic crisis was considered as a new kind of insecurity. Hence, the future treatment of regional security should be reconceptualized, so that there could be better prospects of anticipating future threats from the economic realm. Lastly, the roundtable judged that ASEAN had not fully addressed the implications of the current crisis for the poor. In the light of the tendency of the crisis to push an increasing number of people to become poor, ASEAN cooperation in labour and social protection needed to aim at preventing the crisis from causing further social damage.

The roundtable's programme and a list of the names and contact data of the participants are at the end of this report.

The report begins with a brief background and summarizes the important observations made during the discussions. It includes the recommendations made. This is followed by short papers by Herman Joseph S. Kraft, Yeo Lay Hwee, Kazutoshi Chatani and Kee Beom Kim, Lim Teck Ghee, Hui Cheung Tai, and Raymond Atje and Pratiwi Kartika.

We hope that the summary and the papers will help both policy-makers and the interested public in understanding the impact of the current economic crisis on ASEAN and Southeast Asia as a region.

I
ASEAN ROUNDTABLE 2009

THE GLOBAL
ECONOMIC CRISIS:
IMPLICATIONS FOR ASEAN

ASEAN ROUNDTABLE 2009

THE GLOBAL ECONOMIC CRISIS: IMPLICATIONS FOR ASEAN

Background

The theme of the 2009 Roundtable reflected the current challenges ASEAN faces. The global economic and financial crisis — probably the worst the world has witnessed in the last 100 years — has spared none of the major economic regions. Stock markets have fallen, and GDP growth numbers have been severely downgraded. The impact is now being felt on employment, consumer spending and inflation, with deflationary effects in many countries. Asia, where two of the biggest developing economies — China and India — are located, is also experiencing the consequences of the crisis. As most of the countries in developing Asia are significantly export-oriented, the impact of the slowdown in the United States (U.S.), the European Union (EU) countries and Japan has resulted in sharp contractions in several ASEAN economies in the last few quarters. While governments have undertaken policy changes and several measures to soften the blow and support employment and consumer spending, the effect of these measures are not yet fully evident. However, with the recent emergence of "green shoots" of recovery, financial markets seem to have rallied. The positive news on U.S. financial institutions and the onset of an apparent stimulus to the Chinese economy have benefited ASEAN. It still remains to be seen whether the present situation points to genuine recovery and whether growth could be realistically expected to return to the pre-crisis levels of mid-2007. ASEAN should thus be ready with a preventive coordinated approach to boost economic growth and ease worries on the impact of the crisis.

These sobering thoughts, shared by Ambassador K. Kesavapany, Director of the Institute of Southeast Asian Studies (ISEAS), set the tone for the ASEAN Roundtable 2009, held on 18 June 2009 with the theme "The Global Economic Crisis: Implications for ASEAN". It was jointly organized by the ASEAN Studies Centre at ISEAS with the support of the Konrad Adenauer Stiftung (KAS) at Pan Pacific Hotel, Singapore. KAS has partnered with ISEAS in organizing annual ASEAN Roundtables for the past seven years. The themes of the roundtables address topical issues on ASEAN's agenda, and the outcomes are published as policy reports.

The 2009 Roundtable aimed to study the impact of the current global economic crisis on ASEAN members and its community-building process, assessing it through the lens of regional security, economy and finance, and the social impact. Roundtable sessions involved representatives from the government, the private sector and academia. Some of the leading participants were Herman Kraft of the University of the Philippines-Diliman; Natasha Hamilton-Hart of the National University of Singapore; Yeo Lay Hwee of the European Union Centre in Singapore; Peter Van Rooij of the International Labour Organization, Jakarta; Lim Teck Ghee of the Centre for Policy Initiatives, Malaysia; Lim Chze Cheen of the ASEAN Secretariat; Mohamed Ariff of the Malaysian Institute of Economic Research; Hui Cheung Tai of the Standard Chartered Bank, Singapore; Jaseem Ahmed of the Asian Development Bank; and Raymond Atje of the Centre for Strategic and International Studies, Jakarta. Arin Jira, Chairman of the ASEAN Business Advisory Council, was the distinguished luncheon speaker. The programme and the full list of participants appear in ANNEX I and ANNEX II.

Session I: Strategic and Political Implications

The roundtable's first session addressed two questions:

- How will the crisis affect the realization of the ASEAN Political and Security Community (APSC)?
- Will changes in economic relationships have an impact on existing strategic relationships (within ASEAN and with its dialogue partners)?

The APSC's contribution is most evident in laying the normative foundations for ASEAN. The ASEAN discourse has shifted its language and concerns, opening space for addressing norms such as human rights, governance and democracy. There is some concern over how ASEAN approaches such concepts as "human security", "comprehensive security", "human rights" and "democracy". Human rights as expressed in the APSC and the ASEAN Charter do not seem to be a shared goal for ASEAN, but rather, part of a regional agenda to bring about change at the domestic level. High expectations of the new language of human rights in ASEAN may be misplaced, as interests do not merge on this as with other conventional security concerns.

A related concern is ASEAN's aspiration to be a rule-based community. This may be difficult to achieve as some ASEAN members are not rule-based regimes. ASEAN should examine more closely the discrepancy in the practices espoused on the ground and the norms adopted at the regional level. This is not to belittle the efforts of the APSC, the ASEAN Charter and ASEAN's normative goals, but rather to clarify whether there is real commitment and will to pursue these goals.

As the APSC underpins the normative element in the ASEAN Community, the impact of the crisis on regional political and security issues lies in distracting the focus of ASEAN member states. As it is, the APSC still lacks a clear definition of concepts like democracy and human rights. Preoccupation with the crisis would thus cause further delay in the clarification of and action on these issues.

ASEAN also faces the challenge of reconciling the rhetoric of its commitment to the realization of the APSC with the reality of creating the necessary institutional mechanisms. This institutional weakness is not necessarily a failure or a lapse, as it appears to suit the regional process. However, institution-building under the APSC may be slowed down as member states turn to other concerns.

Nonetheless, the crisis will not stall or halt the APSC's overall processes, albeit slowing its pace. Progress — and its pace — would depend on the will and initiative of the ASEAN member states. The APSC provides a normative platform for ASEAN in a way that earlier commitments do not, where it is:

- A rules-based community of shared values and norms;
- A cohesive, peaceful, stable and resilient region with shared responsibility for comprehensive security; and
- A dynamic and outward-looking region.

In responding to challenges in the political and security sphere, ASEAN's track record seems to indicate that it has often come out stronger from such challenges, as demonstrated during the Cambodian crisis and Vietnam's invasion of Cambodia in the 1970s. However, in situations where there was a confluence of external crisis and internal turmoil, ASEAN responses were not as effective. This could be seen in how ASEAN responded to the 1997–98 Asian financial crisis, when ASEAN countries had largely been preoccupied with domestic issues. Only when domestic situations stabilized at the turn of the twentieth century — in Thailand, Indonesia and Malaysia — did ASEAN activism return, as did the enthusiasm for community-building.

Session I Conclusions

ASEAN does not seem to have a clear-cut response to the security implications of the crisis. This could be due to the compartmentalization of the three ASEAN communities, despite their interlinked nature. While a large part of the APSC's focus is on human security — which implies how changes in the economic and political situations of ASEAN states affect the lives of people — there are few activities in the APSC addressing this. The notion of "human security" itself could be double-edged, as seen in the experiences of Indonesia in 1998 and in Malaysia in 2008 resulting from economic and financial difficulties.

With regard to whether an over-arching regional institution was necessary to address transnational concerns, the general view is that creating such an entity would only add to the institutional noodle bowl in the region without necessarily delivering any substantive results. For example, the East Asia Vision Group's recommendations on community-building in East Asia have not yet been addressed.

At present ASEAN's Dialogue Partners, such as the U.S., the EU, China and India are all preoccupied with their own domestic problems arising from the current crisis. Nonetheless, there is an emerging recognition of ASEAN as a collective entity, as illustrated by the G-20's interest in engaging ASEAN. ASEAN is seeing a re-adjustment of strategic and security relationships, different from the situation in 1997–98.

ASEAN should identify and work on goals and aspiration that are truly common and shared by all members. ASEAN should emphasize with its actions that it is serious about deepening integration. ASEAN members should not use the crisis to delay or slow down implementation of the ASEAN Community Blueprints.

Session II: The Social Consequences

The Roundtable's second session focused on two topics:

*   ASEAN's response mechanisms for labour and social protection: challenges in creating crisis-resilient economies; and
*   What ASEAN could do to address rising poverty levels and social unrest?

ASEAN countries saw a substantial decline in economic activity only after the crisis had intensified in and ravaged its principal markets and sources of investment — the U.S., the EU and Japan. The decline had resulted in growing job losses with implications for future employment opportunities. The situation was aggravated in ASEAN countries with high population growth, and in those already facing youth employment challenges. The rising numbers of workers who have turned to informal and vulnerable employment, including the rural economy, are indicators of working poverty. Added to this is the fall in official aid flows from developed economies, as well as the decline in remittances from migrant workers (a source of income for poor households).

ASEAN members regularly share information on social protection at the regional level; however, there are no coherent regional policies or strategies to strengthen social protection. This can be seen in the outcome of the 14th ASEAN Summit held in February 2009 in Cha-am, Thailand, which placed more emphasis on economic and financial sector responses, rather than on regional poverty and the social impact of the crisis. At both national and regional levels, stimulus packages have given little attention to strengthen social safety nets and social protection programmes. There is no evidence of substantive efforts at formulating and implementing policies that systematically address the problem of rising poverty.

While in the short term macroeconomic policies can help to accelerate recovery and enhance resilience, governments will need to strengthen employment and social protection policies, as labour market recovery lags economic recovery by four or five years. Governments also need to provide support for the vulnerable groups in the labour market, as well as small and medium-sized enterprises, which are the "backbone of employment" and can bolster the growth of a dynamic private sector.

Social protection programmes should be incorporated into economic stimulus packages, which currently lack a social focus. This is important for ASEAN countries, as their social protection systems are in general at an early stage of development. Only Brunei Darussalam has a universal pension scheme. While public sector employees in ASEAN countries (except Cambodia) enjoy social insurance, the general public does not have similar coverage. The vast majority of informal sector workers are excluded from existing social protection (see Table 1.1). ASEAN also needs to work on shifting health financing towards social insurance and universal coverage and expanding unemployment insurance schemes. Social protection should not be seen as a cost but a key investment in human capital.

The crisis presents an opportunity to extend basic social protection to cover all citizens. It is also an opportunity for government and social partners to work together in designing and

TABLE 1.1

Social Protection Schemes in ASEAN Member States

	Brunei	*Cambodia*	*Indonesia*	*Laos*	*Malaysia*	*Myanmar*	*Philippines*	*Singapore*	*Thailand*	*Vietnam*
Old age	P/U		P	S	P		S	P	S	S
Invalidity	P/U		P	S	S/P		S	P	S	S
Survivors	P		P	S	S/P		S	P	S	S
Medical care	U		S	S	U	S	S	P/A	U/S	S
Sickness	E	E	E	S	E		S	E	S	S
Maternity	E	E	E	S	E		S	E	S	S
Work injury	E	S	S	S	S/E	S	S	E	S	S

Note: S: social insurance, P: provident fund, U: universal, E: employer liability, A: social assistance.

Source: Hiroshi Yamabana, "Overview of Social Protection Scheme in Asia Pacific Countries", a presentation delivered at Kuala Lumpur on 19 August 2008.

implementing responsive labour and social protection systems. In strengthening the social dimension of regional integration under the ASEAN Socio-Cultural Community (ASCC), ASEAN should:

- Develop and implement social assistance programmes, such as targeted cash transfers and employment programmes to support the purchasing power of vulnerable households;
- Invest in human capital as a critical driver of competitiveness;
- Collectively seek to establish mechanisms for learning and sharing of information on strengthening social protection and extending it to the informal economy; and
- Involve governments, employers and workers in social protection reform.

The crisis has also affected those who had managed to climb above the poverty line but had now tumbled back below it as a result of the loss of jobs or income arising from the crisis. In a globally connected world, the key issue is how to protect the new middle class from falling back into poverty. With careful targeting, governments can identify the most vulnerable in key socioeconomic and occupational groups affected by the crisis, so that stimulus packages or remedial measures reach the most deserving and needy amongst the traditional and the new poor. Lessons learnt from the 1997–98 crisis and best practices in poverty reduction highlight the importance of good governance; empowerment of the poor, especially women; placing rural poverty alleviation in the context of overall economic growth; promoting off-farm employment; addressing structural imbalances, especially access to land as the basic factor of production; combating graft, leakage and corruption; promoting awareness and access to information and transparency; supporting the facilitating and monitoring role of NGOs; and building local leadership.

National and regional policymakers should focus on developing policies and programmes to respond to the poverty impact of the economic crisis in light of:

- the impact on poverty numbers and poverty levels;
- the major ways in which the poor are affected by the crisis, and the types of remedial measures that can be of greatest benefit to the poor; and
- the complex relationship between poverty, inequality and the larger political economy in the longer run.

Session II Conclusions

In terms of social protection, the issue of migrant workers is an area where a collective ASEAN initiative will make an impact. At present, the ASEAN approach to its regional social agenda tends to be more of a debate on "theological" issues rather than practical solutions. For more effective interventions on poverty reduction, ASEAN will need to change how it formulates and implements its social agenda. As regards measures to get people out of — and to stay out of — poverty, ASEAN countries should achieve greater progress in their microfinance endeavours. Microfinance and micro-insurance would complement social security schemes. As a collective entity, ASEAN would also do well to identify and address the "low-hanging fruit" from the Millennium Development Goals, which are to be achieved by 2015. Reducing child mortality and malnutrition are such "low-hanging fruit". To do so, however, ASEAN should set and abide by time-bound targets to accomplish goals to which countries have collectively committed. 2015 is a feasible realization date, which also coincides with the realization of the ASEAN Community. Finally, the rich countries should act as partners and facilitators, avoiding charitable or handout approaches to poverty alleviation.

Luncheon Speech

Mr Arin Jira, Chairman of the ASEAN Business Advisory Council (ASEAN-BAC), was the distinguished luncheon speaker. He shared the experience of the private sector in doing business in ASEAN. According to him, the current crisis hampered the process of regional integration. The policy alteration and shifts undertaken by governments had shaken the confidence of investors. While multinational companies could still take advantage of the present situation, the small and medium enterprises tended to stay local. He expressed his belief that ASEAN should shift its strategy from reliance on U.S. demand to more on intra-ASEAN trade. This was particularly relevant at a time when countries in the West were introducing measures that had protectionist undertones. Shifting to increased activity with neighbours would, however, require public-private partnerships as an essential factor. This was an area of weakness for ASEAN. ASEAN still lacked a formal mechanism for private sector involvement. Thus, both governments and private sector need to collaborate in helping businesses overcome bureaucratic hurdles.

Mr Arin Jira highlighted the lack of recognition of ASEAN brands. To address this, ASEAN countries need to increase the share of trade and investment among themselves. There should also be initiatives to increase the production and consumption of ASEAN goods and to raise their value. He cited the example of the ASEAN-BAC's initiative of conferring the ASEAN Business Award on outstanding ASEAN companies, thus giving them greater prominence and raising their profile. Similar initiatives or arrangements should be made to encourage SMEs to expand their operations in the region and to attract investments, including venture capital. In turn, successful companies can share the business sector's views on and experience with difficulties encountered as a result of ASEAN's ongoing regionalism efforts.

Mr Arin Jira concluded by calling for greater business interaction to transform the ASEAN region into a regional economic base. He suggested that this could be achieved through greater private-public partnerships. He encouraged ASEAN governments to initiate and create companies, provide direction and guidance, and open up opportunities to invest in the companies. This could be initiated first in the agriculture sector, from which ASEAN countries produce a significant percentage of the region's commodities. He cautioned, however, that cooperation among and within member states was important to regulate supply and demand, so as not to compromise national interests. ASEAN countries could all participate in this endeavour without differentiation. For example countries without natural endowments could contribute skilled labour and infrastructural needs. Mr Arin Jira's concluding advice was for ASEAN to put business "on the right track" as much remained to be done for ASEAN to realize its aspiration of becoming a regional powerhouse.

Session III: Economy and Finance

The third and last session of the Roundtable dealt with three main questions:

- How is ASEAN coping with the economic vulnerabilities that have emerged from the crisis?
- How are the financial and banking sectors in ASEAN faring and coping?
- What would be the implications of this crisis on building an ASEAN Economic Community (AEC) by 2015?

Current ASEAN responses addressing the economic and financial consequences of the crisis include enhancing competitiveness "at", "behind" and "across" the border; consolidating schedules for eliminating tariffs and other barriers to trade and investment; and addressing structural gaps in infrastructure development. However, as implementation moves slowly in ASEAN, the economic initiatives would need to be regularly reported, monitored and evaluated through a "scorecard" system. This is a necessary compliance mechanism to ensure implementation coordination. ASEAN is also working on a feedback channel so that it can have more engagement with the private sector.

ASEAN member states responded individually to the economic crisis, through interest rates and monetary and fiscal policy measures. The crisis, however, is a clear reminder that a more coordinated response is needed at the regional level. Some suggestions for ASEAN are to:

- Rebalance its growth through diversification, relying less on U.S. consumption and diversifying its export markets;
- Promote investment through infrastructure projects, as there is a need for fiscal stimulus to support real economic growth and infrastructure development (for example, through initiatives such as the ASEAN Infrastructure Mechanism);
- Strengthen financial systems and promote financial market development, including the development of a local currency bond market (to reduce dependence on foreign bond markets) and financial services liberalization (to develop and integrate capital markets); and financial integration through information exchanges (to facilitate collective assessment of economic conditions, risks and vulnerabilities); and
- Participate in credible reforms of the global and regional financial architecture and voice ASEAN's position and views on responses. Global fora such as the G-20, International Monetary Fund (IMF), World Trade Organization (WTO) and Bank for International Settlements (BIS) are such venues. In addition, ASEAN should also undertake reforms in key areas, such as regulation and supervision, early warning systems, and regulatory cooperation and coordination. This would assist ASEAN to act promptly and collectively in responding to the changing financial and economic conditions.

While this seems to paint a more or less positive picture, ASEAN countries should not downplay the severity of the global financial and economic crisis. For ASEAN, the impact of the global crisis is felt more in the economic sphere, with falling demand for ASEAN exports. The impact on other spheres of cooperation, however, should not be understated. Although stabilization is now taking place, it will more likely to be a W-shaped recovery rather than the V- , U- or L-shaped recovery that are being predicted. If so, the stimulus packages introduced by governments will not be able to sustain the recovery process, and the contraction will likely be prolonged, possibly lasting up to 2011. Similar to the Great Depression of 1932, protectionism would prolong the recession. ASEAN countries should learn from mistakes, unlike the G-20 nations, who have not heeded those Great Depression lessons and have drawn up such protectionist measures again.

It should also be borne in mind that current ASEAN-wide regional initiatives are not a direct result of the current crisis. These initiatives had been devised much earlier to address the impact of the 1997–98 financial and economic crisis in Asia. With no substantive monetary or fiscal cooperation, ASEAN will be ill-prepared for the next crisis, which is likely to be the collapse of the U.S. dollar. This may cause exchange rate volatility and serious inflation problems, and ASEAN should be prepared to respond to these problems.

However, from the finance and banking sector perspective, the opinion is that Asia's fundamentals are intact and capital flows are better. Asia has not experienced as much deterioration in credibility as developed regions, such as the United States and the European Union, as shown in the recovery of the equity markets to pre-Lehman levels and in the tightening of sovereign credit default swap spreads. Even so, the reduced demand for capital due to a sudden and substantial fall in business activities has reduced the volume of trade finance. Consequently, month-on-month lending has fallen even further. It should also be noted that ASEAN economies do not have the same kind of attraction for capital inflow as their North Asian counterparts. Another pertinent point is the rapid development of Islamic banking in Asia, which requires ASEAN to include this in its economic plans. Overall, ASEAN countries will face three challenges in the financial and banking sector:

- Deterioration in credit quality brought about by slower economic growth:
  i. Non-performing loan ratios are expected to rise on account of the slowdown in growth and the difficult business environment.
  ii. ASEAN banks' strong growth and limited exposure allow them to reduce leverage and improve profitability and liquidity.
- Capital flow returning to Asia leading to asset overvaluation:
  i. Investors will look to re-enter select ASEAN markets, as risk appetite improves and they regain confidence in the region's economic and currency outlook.
  ii. Prompt intervention by authorities is needed to limit volatility.
- Change in the regulatory landscape in Asia, particularly to ensure responsible consumer finance practices:
  i. Ensuring adequate capital, quality and quantity.
  ii. Further ingraining risk management culture into governance.
  iii. Extending the reach of regulation across products, financial institutions and geographies.
  iv. Increasing international coordination.

Regulatory action is required to further mitigate risks. The U.S. policy response in the aftermath of the Lehman crisis was immediate and unconventional, with a significant expansion in the Federal Reserve's balance sheet. The Fed stood as the lender of last resort for U.S. banks and simultaneously offered swap lines for other central banks globally, including in Asia. As a result, stock prices and exchange rates stabilized. However, bond yields and the cost of government access to market finance are still high. The downturn is expected to be prolonged in the EU countries, the United States and Japan. The policy response to the financial crisis in the United States has been effective so far, but could prove to be inadequate in the medium term. As a result, banks would be operating on borrowed time until the end of 2009. It remains to be seen how the market will react in a situation when there is no longer government intervention. Recent market events can prove to be a "false dawn" despite indications that a normal level of risk appetite is returning. The G-7 sovereign borrowing spreads are still rising. Yet, bond yields continue to fall in Asia, which implies a rising risk appetite in Asia in preference of the United States or the European Union. However, it is still too early to gauge whether this is sustainable.

As to whether the global crisis will cause serious delays for realizing the AEC by 2015, the panoply of agreements and responses makes it difficult for outsiders to adequately monitor and verify AEC implementation. ASEAN will have to remove many barriers behind and at the border if the AEC blueprint is to be realized. Furthermore, the ASEAN Secretariat currently lacks the capacity to undertake the tasks expected of it. The peer review mechanism is also seen as ineffective. There are a number of reasons for ASEAN countries to delay the implementation of the AEC blueprint:

• Intense domestic pressure stops or even reverses economic reforms. Economic reforms lead to a reallocation of resources from one group to another. It is politically tempting to give in to the "losers".

- Member countries do not consider the implementation of the blueprint as their top priority. The current crisis could be used as an excuse to defer further reforms. If so, the damage to the reputation of ASEAN and regional cooperation will be long-lasting.

Thus, an independent body should monitor AEC implementation. The ASEAN Secretariat is not independent in this sense, as it is the secretariat for an intergovernmental organization and relies on the inputs of government agencies. These agencies may have their own interests (or reasons) not to reveal the actual status of implementation, even with the scorecard system. In addition, officials may be motivated to prevent the disclosure of reports that are detrimental to their countries' interest and may instead provide a watered-down version of the actual implementation status and problems.

Session III Conclusions

Generally, it can be said that for the economy and finance sectors:

- ASEAN has had a rough ride but has shown resilience;
- The region has avoided severe damage due to reforms undertaken earlier; and
- Even though credit default swaps have risen, this is primarily reflective of risk aversion and not of the fundamentals.

The MNCs' view of the slow pace of progress in ASEAN is reflected in the business sector's opinion that ASEAN needs to have a sense of urgency. ASEAN must also speed up AEC implementation. As the traditional markets are drying up, MNCs are looking for new markets, which, in the present situation, are China, India, Russia, Vietnam and Indonesia. ASEAN should start working on creating a business-friendly environment in the region, and not wait for 2015 to act.

The U.S. regulatory structure has helped it avoid three out of five crises. For ASEAN, regulations are such that it tries to prevent five of next the three crises, with tight control measures such as those being imposed on the banking sector and capital markets. As this is a comprehensive crisis, which requires consistent rules across markets, institutions and instruments, every highly leveraged institution must be highly regulated by a prudent regulator. All this will mean low profitability of banks and a new financial architecture. Institutions will have to be less complex and smaller instead of the pre-crisis conglomerates.

When the current crisis is over, the world will not go back to its previous growth rate. There will be a global imbalance as the past driver of economic growth — U.S. consumption — will go down. This must be addressed, that is, the East must save less and spend more, and the United States must spend less and save more. This is where ASEAN can play a very important role, by putting into place a mechanism for the ASEAN+3 (East Asia) to be the driver of growth.

Some principles should also be set for risk management but with room for flexibility. After the crisis, there will be much criticism of Western regulation. But some degree of synchronization and coordination is still needed across all financial markets. Finally, for Asia (and ASEAN) a coordinated approach within the region is more effective than individual countries working on their own.

Conclusions and Policy Suggestions

Participants felt that the crisis has a significant impact on the region, and ASEAN needs to have a better coordinated approach if it has to weather the storm. This has to be in the form of both regulatory reform of the financial sector, with more oversight by the central banks, and policy actions to kick-start growth and employment as well as sustain them through the recovery stage.

The region in particular has to remember that the developed countries and regions like the United States and the EU will take a long time to heal the scars of the crisis, notwithstanding the "green shoots" of recovery that are visible today. Hence, while export-led growth policies have served the region well, governments will now have to think of policies that are oriented more towards domestic or regional markets. This could take the form of more spending on infrastructure development, among others. Anticipating the immediate future and responses is thus crucial for ASEAN. The right actions will ensure that capital continues to flow into the region, both as direct investments and into the financial markets, signalling confidence in the region's governance.

One of the main findings of this conference is that the notion of "security" is not definite, and can be ambiguous at times. Countries in the region have frequently explained away the source of insecurity in political and military terms, overlooking other aspects of regional "insecurities". The current economic crisis, considered as a new kind of insecurity, has hit the countries in the region hard. Many initially failed to respond coherently to the crisis, let alone attempt to really understand the nature of the crisis. Hence, future treatment of the issue of regional security should be reconceptualized so that it could anticipate the possibility of future threats that may emerge from the economic realm.

As ASEAN countries continue to grapple with the impact of the crisis, the region must also be ready to implement measures that will minimize the negative impact of the crisis on the most vulnerable groups. ASEAN has not fully addressed the social — particularly the poverty — implications of the current crisis. This is a cause for concern, as the region has recently seen job losses in critical sectors. Given the increasing tendency of the crisis to push many people in several ASEAN countries into poverty — including the most affected groups, such as the existing poor, youths, migrant workers and their families — ASEAN cooperation in labour and social protection needs to take bold steps now to prevent the crisis from causing further social damage.

II
BACKGROUND
PAPERS

1
THE ASEAN POLITICAL-SECURITY COMMUNITY AND THE FINANCIAL CRISIS

Herman Joseph S. Kraft

Introduction

This paper looks at how the global financial crisis impacts on the ASEAN aspiration to build an ASEAN Community. In particular, it looks at the crisis' effect on the establishment of an ASEAN Political-Security Community (APSC). It argues three points. First, the most important contribution of the APSC is in the normative foundations it outlines for ASEAN. These foundations are first and foremost directed at ensuring domestic stability and harmony, but it has its principal objective in strengthening ASEAN's position in East Asian regionalism and in maintaining security in Southeast Asia and the broader context of the Asia-Pacific region. The normative commitments outlined in the APSC, however, also imply the need for a certain degree of institutionalization — an outcome that ASEAN does not seem to be as committed to. This brings out the second point — ASEAN, despite its rhetorical commitment to a particular set of normative structures, will continue to be bogged down in setting up the institutional mechanisms needed to realize these normative structures. Third, the intra-ASEAN dynamics at the centre of this issue will be further complicated by the effects of the global financial crisis. In general, ASEAN will continue to be burdened by the inherent contradiction between the normative aspirations expressed in the APSC Blueprint and its desire to maintain existing institutional structural arrangements.

The ASEAN Political-Security Community

On 3 June 2003, Rizal Sukma of the Centre for Strategic and International Studies in Jakarta presented a paper conceptualizing an ASEAN security community at a seminar, "ASEAN Cooperation: Challenges and Prospects in the Current International Situation". Sukma pointed to the need for the establishment of an ASEAN security community that would pursue a comprehensive framework of security that gives equal importance to both traditional and non-military security issues and responses (Sukma 2003, p. 3). The paper was conceived in reaction to the proposal of the Singaporean Government to establish an ASEAN Economic Community (AEC) that went beyond the ASEAN Free Trade Area (AFTA). Sukma argued that "ASEAN can no longer pretend that peace, stability, and prosperity can only be achieved through economic cooperation" (Sukma 2003, p. 2). This paper eventually became the departure point for the Indonesian Government's initiative on the establishment of the ASEAN Security Community.

The establishment of the ASC as part of a projected ASEAN Community was formalized in the Declaration of ASEAN Concord II, or Bali Concord II. In this document, the reference to the ASC re-emphasized a number of fundamental norms that ASEAN defines as being essential to its identity as a long-standing regional association. These include (Bali II 2003):

1.   The continued subscription to comprehensive security with its recognition of the interconnectedness of political, economic and sociocultural realities;

2.   Respect for national sovereignty and non-interference in the internal affairs of other countries;

3.   Consensus-based decision-making; and

4.   The renunciation of the use or threat of the use of force, and peaceful settlement of disputes and differences.

It made the outright claim, however, that some issues, particularly maritime issues, are transboundary in nature and require a regional response. This, in fact, is the starting point for the rationale behind the ASC: the need to intensify ASEAN cooperation in areas of security where self-help is insufficient as an approach. To this end, Bali Concord II specifically mentions that the members of ASEAN are committed to strengthening regional and national capacities to address terrorism, trafficking in drugs, persons and other transnational crimes.

The more detailed provisions contained in the Vientiane Action Programme (VAP) fundamentally followed from the Bali Concord II and from what the framers of the ASC had originally intended. The VAP stated that the concept of the ASC affirms ASEAN's adherence to comprehensive security. This is a perspective of security which holds to the idea of the interdependence between the political, economic and social life of the region. To this end, its foundational elements include political and social stability, economic prosperity, narrowed development gap, poverty alleviation and the reduction of social disparity. Thus, even as ASEAN continued to commit itself under the ASC Plan of Action to addressing issues that reflect typical security concerns (for example, the implementation of the Declaration on the Conduct of Parties on the South China Sea, military exchanges and cooperation short of a formal defence agreement, counter-terrorism, counter-insurgency and concerns regarding the maintenance of territorial integrity and respect for national sovereignty), it also noted the need to adopt policies in relation to non-traditional security issues such as transnational crime and other transboundary problems, maritime security cooperation, law enforcement cooperation, and cooperation on environmental problems. Beyond this dichotomy between traditional and non-traditional security, however, the ASC Plan of Action in the VAP also specifically committed the ASEAN states to the establishment of a peaceful region in the context of "a just, *democratic*, and harmonious environment" (VAP 2004, p. 6). Key to this is the need to pursue such issues as democratization, human rights promotion (and even outright protection in the case of women, children and migrant workers), and post-conflict peace-building.

The APSC Blueprint which was accepted by the ASEAN leaders on 1 March 2009, fundamentally follows from the general outline of the ASEAN Security Community Plan of Action in the VAP. Turning it into the ASEAN Political Security Community, however, is a recognition of what has been clear in the VAP — the ASEAN Security Community Action Plan gives expression to the broader political aspirations of ASEAN rather than a strictly security one. Another way of arguing it is that the envisaged security community very clearly goes beyond the traditional understanding of security (as Sukma had originally noted it should). Fundamentally, the APSC promotes the establishment of:

1.   A rules-based community of shared values and norms;
2.   A cohesive, peaceful, stable and resilient region with shared responsibility for comprehensive security; and
3.   A dynamic and outward-looking region in an increasingly integrated and interdependent world.

It again emphasizes the idea that ASEAN must strive towards a regional environment of justice, democracy and harmony among its members and its people. The APSC is intended to be the means by which greater cooperation between its member countries can be achieved in order to attain higher levels of political development. It is in this context, however, that the APSC significantly moves beyond the ASC Action Plan.

Even as the latter emphasized the need to promote democracy and human rights, it was limited by the injunction that ASEAN must act in concert only in those areas where there is already a consensus. Thus, the VAP limits the action plan on human rights to the protection of women and children's rights since all the members of ASEAN have already acceded to or ratified the Convention on the Elimination of Discrimination against Women and the Convention on the Rights of the Child. In fact, prior to the inception of the ASEAN Charter, ASEAN had already formally sought the assistance of the informal Regional Working Group on the Establishment of an ASEAN Human Rights Mechanism. The ASEAN foreign ministers had tasked the working group to assist in the drafting of a blueprint for a regional mechanism for the protection of women's and children's rights, as well as looking into a mechanism for migrant workers rights in the region. The ratification of the ASEAN Charter, however, superseded all of these.

The APSC Blueprint, with guidance from the charter's provisions, now includes the promotion and protection of human rights in general — not just women's and children's rights. To implement this, the charter commits ASEAN to the establishment of a regional human rights body the terms of reference for which is currently being drafted by a high level panel. In discussions during the drafting of the ASEAN Charter up to the present, the establishment of a regional human rights body has been the highlight of the charter — a highlight that has overridden all other considerations. In fact, civil society groups were critical of the charter because it fell short of expectations raised prior to and during the drafting process (see Kraft 2007). They were willing, however, to overlook the problems because of the perceived advantages that the provisions on human rights in the charter provided.

While the human rights provisions in the charter and, by extension, in the APSC are important, there are other aspects present in both documents that provide possible spaces for advancing advocacy on security sector reform. One is the commitment to the establishment of a rules-based community of shared values and norms. In particular, the opportunities emerge not just from the commitment to promote and protect human rights, but even more so from the commitment to establish a community subordinated to the principles of democracy and good governance. Another is the openings implicit in what is an emerging shift in the security framework in ASEAN. The APSC makes clear the continuing commitment of ASEAN to a comprehensive framework of security.

As has been mentioned before, comprehensive security presupposes the interconnectedness of economic, political and social concerns, and that these may be sources of insecurity as much as the military threats from which states are supposed to protect their citizens. However, while comprehensive security largely emphasized national resilience and attention to the development of national capacities, the security issues that the ASEAN states identify as being central to their concerns increasingly require a regional approach, and, more importantly, go beyond strictly state concerns. At the same time, however, the opportunities provided by these same spaces are not very clear as they face continuing challenges from long-standing ASEAN practices and attitudes.

Providing a Normative Platform for ASEAN

As noted earlier, the ASEAN Charter makes very clear normative commitments to democracy, the rule of law and good governance, and the promotion and protection of human rights. In the APSC Blueprint, the member states of ASEAN are charged with establishing a standard of common adherence to "norms of good conduct among member states of the ASEAN Community; consolidating and strengthening ASEAN's solidarity, cohesiveness and harmony; and contributing to the building of a peaceful, democratic, tolerant, participatory and transparent community in Southeast Asia" (APSC 2009, p. 3). To further the development of common norms and shared values, it incorporates a number of specific action measures. Among these, the following general categories are of particular importance:

Increased Consultation outside of Formal ASEAN Networks

Section A.1 (especially the provisions in numbers 5 and 6) of the APSC contains items and proposed action measures that are directed towards increasing the involvement of entities outside ASEAN's formal networks to its formal processes. These include specific references to increasing the engagement with civil society groups, the private sector and academic networks. ASEAN has been noted for its networking activities among the ASEAN states and with their dialogue partners. Since 1996, however, there has been a notable increase in direct involvement between ASEAN as a body and its different processes with civil society groups within the region. Significantly, the most extensive engagement has perhaps revolved around the establishment of a regional human rights body.

What this engagement has wrought, however, is an emerging habit of consultation with different groups outside the formal networks of ASEAN on different issues, including the issue of ASEAN itself. The drafting of the charter was replete with numerous consultations, from the work of the Eminent Persons Group, to the High Level Task Force, to the continuing discussions on the different blueprints. Admittedly, these engagements are uneven across countries. While civil society involvement in these processes are encouraged and supported in Indonesia, the Philippines, Thailand, and, to an increasing degree, Malaysia and Vietnam, there is still hesitation in involving these groups in Singapore and Laos. In Myanmar and Brunei, there is hardly any consultation taking place outside of the formal institutions of government.

Greater Exchange of and the Free Flow of Information

The provisions in the APSC Blueprint on this particular area fundamentally call for greater openness between and within the ASEAN member states. (In particular, see Section A.1.2 of the APSC Blueprint.) This covers an extensive range of activities which are largely projections at the moment but once implemented would have significant influence over developments in ASEAN. The initial effort has to do with exchanging information on national laws and political systems. Beyond this, however, the APSC Blueprint enjoins the different member countries to facilitate the free flow of information within each country. The implications of the provisions on this particular point are significant as far as debating democracy and good governance is concerned. Again, the limitation is that the injunction is held back by the proviso that this be done within the limits of the different laws and regulations of each country. On the other hand, these injunctions are clear opportunities that could be used to promote greater levels of democracy to be practised in the different member states of ASEAN. These are also openings into a more liberal way of enforcing the long-standing ASEAN adherence to the principle of non-interference.

Encouragement of Activities that would Promote Good Governance, the Protection and Promotion of Human Rights, and the Principles of Democracy

The APSC Blueprint promotes the implementation of a number of general measures in direct relation to good governance, human rights and democracy. There is a specific item on combating and preventing corruption, but to a large extent this is all part of ensuring good governance. All of these recommended actions that could be undertaken could be the basis for initiatives that could be advanced by different groups. The existence of more liberal governments means that there are institutional spaces that could be utilized to promote these activities in order to really make these aspirations meaningful. A key issue here is the ASEAN Human Rights Body. The Terms of Reference document for this institution is still being drafted, but already there are dangerous indications that this body will again be more of a showcase than an actual prize.[1]

The regional aspect to all these activities is concerned with how they could contribute to regional peace and stability. Even as the activities and the goals they are directed at are discrete, they are all part of an overall framework to strengthen cooperation that would enhance the security of the region — an important aspect of which is the further reduction of the prospects for conflict. This refers not only to interstate conflict among the ASEAN states (which is already minimal even with the skirmishes that take place at the Thai-Cambodia, the Thai-Myanmar borders and the fishing lanes in the South China Sea and the tri-border area between Indonesia, Malaysia and the Philippines), but to interstate conflict among the major powers and intra-state conflict which could overspill into inter- and extra-ASEAN state relations.

The APSC Blueprint provides specific action programmes designed to facilitate widespread dissemination and sharing of these norms beyond bureaucratic elites. Regular consultations and institutionalized engagements are increasingly becoming a regular part of ASEAN processes. All these processes, however, do not guarantee change over the short term. Very little has been done by ASEAN regarding continuing political repression in Myanmar, specifically the cases of Daw Aung San Suu Kyi and the Rohingyas. Embedded political elite cynicism and opportunism across the region has allowed corruption, criminality, and other forms of political repression to prosper. More generally, there is still a lack of clear-cut cooperative activities addressing the economic gaps within ASEAN.

It has to be noted that it has been less than two years since the charter was signed by the leaders of the ASEAN states and a few months since its ratification. If we look at it in terms of the APSC Blueprint, the time element becomes even shorter. It is obviously premature (if not outright unfair) to make judgments. It is not, however, so much what has been and has not been accomplished through the charter or the APSC Blueprint that is really telling. The problem is that the institutional mechanisms that would be responsible for making the normative aspirations presented in the charter and the APSC Blueprint a reality continue to be weak. In particular, two interrelated issue areas regarding its institutions continue to keep the sceptics on ASEAN sceptical.

Binding Decisions

A rules-based environment emerges from both procedural and substantive aspects of decision-making. Rules or decisions made must be clear to all and agreements reached must be made on the basis of good faith, that is, that there is the intention to comply. The implication is that decisions are made to apply to all.

By and large, the binding nature of decisions made at the level of ASEAN had in the past been less of an issue because of the consensual process of ASEAN decision-making. Because a consensus approach meant that decisions could only be made on issue areas where the member states of ASEAN were largely in agreement, it had prevented sensitive concerns from becoming divisive issues and thereby contributed to ASEAN solidarity over the years. Due to its consensus approach to decision-making, however, the language in ASEAN declarations tend to be less than explicit about commitments.

The less-than-binding nature of decisions presents continuing problems for ASEAN in relation to the case of Myanmar. The commitment to democracy and human rights that is part of the progressive aspects of the charter, and the action plans specified in the APSC Blueprint only becomes meaningful if there is a serious intent to put into place mechanisms that will allow for the enforcement of human rights protection across the region. There are serious questions regarding the intention to take obligations on human rights that the charter imposes on the ASEAN member states seriously.

Compliance and Sanctions

The seriousness with which states take their obligations under the Charter seriously would have more credibility if there were very clear structures for ensuring compliance. Criticisms directed by ASEAN governments at the military junta for its actions against its own citizens (for example, excessive violence against demonstrators and the political persecution of Aung San Suu Kyi have been the constant bone of contention between the junta and its partners in ASEAN) have been brushed aside, and calls for political reform have at best been met with polite insouciance and less than sincere promises.

Considerations of ASEAN solidarity, however, have taken precedence over substantive concerns that may affect the credibility of ASEAN norms and values, and what the ASEAN Community stands for. Early in the process of the work of the High Level Task Force drafting the charter, it was decided that provisions on discipline would be left out of the charter to make the language less divisive.[2] Instead, a provision was included that referred questions of discipline regarding cases of serious breach of the charter or cases of non-compliance on provisions of agreements to the ASEAN Summit. This effectively gives the state involved a veto on what should be done to it. The charter's insistence on referring such matters to the ASEAN Summit, with its decision-making via consensus approach, negates the effect of the inclusion of even a weak reference to addressing non-compliance.

The Global Financial Crisis and Southeast Asia

The emergence of the global financial crisis creates a different wrinkle in the prospective development of the APSC. To be clear about it, the issues related to the APSC presented above are concerns that preceded the global financial crisis. The crisis, however, can at best provide a distraction and at worst an excuse from seriously undertaking the action programmes of the APSC.

At the end of 2008, there was a general sigh of relief and a sense that the impact of the global financial crisis on Asian economies was going to be less virulent than the effects of the 1997 crisis (*The Economist* 2008, pp. 35–36). At that point, there were significant downturns in the economies of the countries in the region, but without the sense of panic that emerged in the case of more than ten years ago. By the middle of 2009, however, some countries in the region had been hit hard by the global economic slowdown. High levels of exposure to the global financial markets and consumer markets have made them vulnerable over time to the lingering effects of the crisis. Singapore is expecting a contraction in its economy by as much as 5 per cent, and projections for Thailand indicate a –2 per cent growth to be likely. Malaysia's dependence on exports has likewise made it vulnerable to the effects of the global economic downturn. The Philippines' dependence on the remittances of overseas workers (particularly those from the economically strapped North American states) and its high debt to GDP ratio also puts it in a difficult situation (*The Economist* 2009a, p. 70; *Far Eastern Economic Review* 2009, pp. 13–16). Vietnam expects that its economic growth will slow down to 3.2 per cent from the previous year's 6.1 per cent. Among the large countries in the region, only Indonesia has been able to keep its head above water (*The Economist* 2009b, pp. 26–27).

ASEAN does not have a good record of responding collectively to crises situation affecting its members over the last fifteen years. Its impotence during the crisis of 1997–98 was the subject of much introspection over the future of the grouping. Subsequent developments wherein ASEAN was not able to decisively play a leading role in resolving issues such as the violence that came with the independence of Timor Leste from Indonesia, the haze, and the case of the Rohingyas have only served to confirm this problem. Given its institutional issues, this is not likely to be resolved over the short term. It is thus unlikely that ASEAN will be a major factor in the strategies of countries in the region out of the current crisis. The question here, however, is what does this poor record on crisis management portend for the prospects of the ASEAN Political-Security Community? On this point, the effect of the global financial crisis can be seen in two ways.

The first is more direct, but less decisive in terms of its effects on ASEAN progress on the establishment of the APSC. This refers to the material effects of the crisis — the economic costs involved in trying to counter the effects of the crisis. As noted above, the Indonesian economy has demonstrated its resilience in being able to get through the current crisis — the opposite of what happened in 1997–98. A major factor here is the stimulus package of US$6 billion that the Indonesian Government had put together. This constitutes 1.4 per cent of the country's GDP in 2008. The Singaporean Government on the other hand announced that it would put into place a stimulus package that would be worth 8 per cent of its GDP. Other governments have similar policies that would mean increased government spending. In a situation where domestic economic conditions require the full attention of those in positions of authority, international concerns (short of war or conflict with other states) tend to be given less priority if not set aside completely. In the case of ASEAN, its intergovernmental nature implies that participation in regional programmes depends on the willingness and capacity of governments. A number of the action programmes recommended in the APSC Blueprint point to increased intra-ASEAN involvement — exchanges, educational and training activities, and capacity-building. With the crisis, governments will be too distracted to seriously engage in community-building, especially one that involves normative commitments that go against the existing political conditions.

The issue of normative commitments leads to the second point. The APSC Blueprint calls for activities that will promote democratization and human rights protection, the rule of law, and good governance. This is an area which arguably has more strategic implications for ASEAN than the material aspect of the financial crisis. As noted previously, the most significant aspect of the APSC Blueprint are the action programmes directed at establishing the normative foundation it lays out for ASEAN. More specifically, its emphasis on enhancing ASEAN cooperation to "strengthen democracy, enhance good governance and the rule of law, and to promote and protect human rights and fundamental freedoms, with due regard to the rights and responsibilities of the member states of ASEAN, so as to ultimately create a Rules-based Community of shared values and norms" presents a picture of the direction ASEAN would like to take in its future development.

These, however, express aspirations and not real conditions on the ground. The ASEAN states remain a diverse grouping of different peoples with different economic and political systems. Pursuing a course that promotes democratization, and making the commitment to promote and protect human rights are not decisions that would come easily to all its members. This is why the issues on decision-making and compliance are major institutional gaps that need to be reconciled with the inherent reticence of some ASEAN member states in initiating a process that would lead to political change in their countries. The financial crisis provides a distraction in terms of the allocation of resources assuming that there is a sincere desire to pursue the aspirations laid out in the APSC Blueprint. The assumption of a "sincere desire", however, is not an easy one to make considering past experience. If there is no "sincere desire" to initiate the process that would lead towards the APSC with all its normative structures intact, then the financial crisis would present an excellent opportunity to stall and delay. Human rights issues, for instance, remain with the continuing concerns over Myanmar (with the arrest and trial of Aung San Suu Kyi), and the forced relocation of families living in Phnom Penh as the cash-strapped government turns to real estate developers as part of its capital generation.

On the other hand, however, there can be no expectation of the ASEAN states delaying for too long. Having set the target for the establishment of the ASEAN Community by 2015, they have set a clear point of advocacy for civil society groups as well as government personalities who are intent in seeing the process through. With ASEAN governments and civil society engagement largely institutionalized, it can be expected that the ASEAN member states will be constantly reminded of their commitments. The days of sweeping these issues under the rug have largely gone by. In the end, the current financial crisis will probably present opportunities to stall for those who are not intent on taking their commitments seriously, but it also provides opportunities for those who would like to ensure that the ASEAN states are kept honest about those same commitments.

Notes

1.   During a consultation held in Makati in March 2009, Ambassador Rosario G. Manalo, the Philippine representative to the high-level panel drafting the Terms of Reference (TOR) for the ASEAN Human Rights Body acknowledged that the TOR states that the regional body is supposed to be consultative in nature. Despite her argument that this merely refers to the consultative nature of ASEAN processes and not to the relationship between the body and ASEAN itself, this is an ingenuous distinction at best.

2.   This was explained by Ambassador Manalo, then the Philippine
     delegate to the High Level Task Force drafting the ASEAN Charter,
     during a talk at the University of the Philippines on 6 September
     2007.

References

Association of Southeast Asian Nations. "Declaration of ASEAN Concord
     II (Bali Concord II)". Jakarta: ASEAN Secretariat, 2003.
————. "Vientiane Action Program". Jakarta: ASEAN Secretariat, 2004.
————. "The ASEAN Political-Security Blueprint". Jakarta: ASEAN
     Secretariat, 2009.
Green, David Jay. "Too Little, Too Late". *Far Eastern Economic Review*
     (March 2009): 13–16.
Kraft, Herman Joseph S. "A Charter for ASEAN: Challenges and
     Prospects". Paper presented at the Sentosa Roundtable held on
     16–17 January 2008, Sentosa, Singapore.
————. "Sittin' on the Dock of a Bay". *The Economist*, 22 November
     2008, pp. 35–36.
————. "Troubled Tigers". *The Economist*, 31 January 2009a, pp. 67–70.
————. "So Far So Good". The Economist, 10 January 2009b, pp. 26–27.
Sukma, Rizal. "The Future of ASEAN: Towards a Security Community".
     Unpublished paper presented at a seminar on "ASEAN Cooperation:
     Challenges and Prospects in the Current International Situation"
     held in New York on 3 June 2003.

*Herman Joseph S. Kraft is the Executive Director of the Institute
for Strategic and Development Studies. He is also an Assistant
Professor of the Department of Political Science at University of
the Philippines, Diliman, Quezon City.*

2
WILL CHANGES IN ECONOMIC RELATIONSHIPS HAVE AN IMPACT ON EXISTING STRATEGIC RELATIONSHIPS?

Yeo Lay Hwee

Introduction

The global financial crisis that began with the loss of confidence in the sub-prime mortgages in the second half of 2007 has spiralled into a full blown economic crisis with severe impact on the real economies all around the world. Debates over the causes and consequences of this global crisis, which is no longer confined to the financial sector, continued even as "green shoots" of recovery are said to be appearing. What this paper will attempt to do is to focus on how this global economic crisis has changed the geo-economic and geopolitical landscape in Southeast Asia, and how these in turn will impact ASEAN's own internal economic cooperation. Also to be discussed in the paper will be the impact the global economic crisis has on the ASEAN+3 process, and ASEAN's relations with the European Union (EU). The paper will also draw from the lessons of the Asian financial crisis and ASEAN's responses to this earlier crisis, and speculate on some of the likely outcomes of the current crisis on ASEAN's development of its regional processes and dialogue partnership.

Economic Impact of Global Crisis on Asia and ASEAN

The global impact of the crisis has seen world trade contracted for the first time since World War II. WTO is forecasting that global trade will decline 9 per cent or more in 2009. Till end of 2008 and early 2009, the picture was bleak. Growth has slowed considerably in all emerging economies and gone negative for several of the developed economies. Japan's GDP contracted by 3.3 per cent, the Euro Zone by 1.5 per cent and the United States by 1 per cent in the last quarter of 2008. China which has enjoyed double digit growth for many years, would see growth down to 5–6 per cent in 2009. More broadly, what the crisis has done is to undermine the drivers of globalization — open markets, foreign direct investments and private ownership — and there is a risk of protectionist backlash and economic fragmentation.

In the early stages of the financial crisis in 2007, Asia was spared significant fallout leading to several economists hailing the "decoupling" of the Asian economies from the U.S. locomotive. This was proven wrong as the crisis deepened and developed into a global financial and economic crisis. As noted in the *IMF Survey* magazine, the impact of the global economic crisis on Asia "has been swifter and often deeper than for other regions, partly because of Asia's export dependence and close integration into the global economy" (*IMF Survey Online* 2009, p. 1). The collapse in demand for exports has dealt a heavy blow on the export-driven economies of Asia. The fact that Asia is far more integrated in its supply chain network meant a "contagion" effect that spread rapidly across the region when the demand from advanced economies dropped. A reflection of the severity of the impact of this global crisis on Asia is shown in figures provided by IMF — that between

September 2008 and February 2009, merchandise exports fell at an annualized rate of about 70 per cent in emerging Asia — almost three times more than during the Asian crisis in the later 1990s. Overall, the IMF expects growth for Asia to decelerate to 1.3 per cent in 2009 from 5.1 per cent in 2008 and growth will return to Asia when the global economy recovers.

Within ASEAN, as noted by Gregory Lopez, initially there was a feeling that the crisis was a problem for the rich countries and that they would weather the storm better because of the economic reforms and structural changes in the financial sector undertaken during the Asian financial crisis of the late 1990s. Indeed, most ASEAN countries were enjoying current account surpluses and rapidly accumulating foreign exchange reserves. Budget deficits in many of these countries were modest and there were no cases of serious financial collapse or bank runs. Hence, in Southeast Asia, except for Singapore, the impact and extent of the crisis may not have been fully appreciated. The rapid decline in world trade and the flight to safety in capital markets are however beginning to sink in and growth in Southeast Asia as a whole will contract from 5.2 per cent in 2008 to close to zero in 2009 (Lopez 2009).

Southeast Asia was at the epicentre for the last major Asian financial crisis but is today an innocent bystander suffering the consequences of the financial meltdown in the West. According to Hal Hill, while its relative openness to trade means greater vulnerability to fall in global trade volumes, and the global economic crisis "will inflict some economic distress and social hardship, its effects on the region are likely to be contained" (Hill 2009, p. 2). That said, the greater geopolitical implications of the crisis and how ASEAN responds to these challenges would determine whether ASEAN would be taken seriously in its strategic relations with its Northeast Asian partners, the United States and European Union.

Geopolitical and Geo-economic Implications of the Global Economic Crisis

The West in Decline

The "decline" of the West and the "rise" of Asia had been very much in the literature since the 1990s. The Asian financial crisis and the resurgence of the U.S. economy in the first few years of the twenty-first century dampen the euphoria about the impending arrival of the Asian century. However, the continued rise of China as an economic and political driver of the global economy, together with the rise of India and India's increasing integration into the global economy in the last decade have again fuelled the talk about an Asian global era. The current global financial crisis as Dominique Moisi put it, "will accelerate the comparative decline of the West as a force today and as a model for the rest of the world tomorrow" (Moisi in *ST*, 8 October 2008). While United States remained the only superpower in the military sense, the global financial crisis has further damaged America's reputation (eroded already by the Iraq War and the abuses in Abu Ghraib and Guantanamo Bay) and capacity for world leadership.

Roger Altman in an article in *Foreign Affairs* argued that the financial and economic crash of 2008 is a "major political geopolitical setback for the US and Europe" and it has stripped Washington and European governments of the resources and credibility they need to maintain their role in global affairs. While "these weaknesses may eventually be repaired, in the interim, they will accelerate trends that are shifting the world's center of gravity away from the United States". China will be a major beneficiary of this power shift because of its strong finances — a budget surplus, a current account surplus and nearly US$2 trillion in foreign exchange reserves (Altman 2009).

China on the Rise

While there is no doubt that China will also be adversely affected by the crisis, it will still be able to maintain moderate economic growth through the global crisis. Most important of all, as Altman rightly highlighted, is that fortunately for China, its strong finances and large reserves have meant China has the means to maintain stability in its own financial system and to stimulate its domestic economy. The real economy remains relatively strong and hence, China is now seen as a major economic locomotive to fuel economic recovery.

The rise of China has been a phenomenon discussed for more than a decade now and with the current economic crisis "impairing" the capacity of the West to act, we are perhaps on the verge of a new episode with China's return to its historically central role in the global political economy. However, the fact also remains that China's trade and investments have recorded sharp drops in the last two quarters and about twenty million workers have lost their jobs since the crisis hit. Hence, maintaining steady economic growth to ensure social and political stability remains China's central priority. The aggressive policy response with a US$586 billion stimulus package to support domestic demand and maintain growth is seen as necessary to generate jobs consistent with social stability. China's main focus is still its domestic economy and as Premier Wen Jiabao put it, "steady and fast growth of China's economy is in itself an important contribution to global financial stability" (quoted in Parello-Plesner 2009).

China's rise may not necessarily mean that it is ready to shoulder the responsibility of providing global public goods. But at the regional level, China may be poised to exert greater influence in Southeast Asia. China's actions to further its leadership role in the region include a US$10 billion investment cooperation fund and an offer of US$15 billion in credit to Southeast Asian neighbours. These are aimed at helping countries weather the current crisis. The fund will finance infrastructure development linking China and its neighbours while the loans will be offered as rescue packages over the next three to five years (Bezlova 2009).

G-2 in the Making?

With the way that the U.S. economy and Chinese economy are intertwined like Siamese twins, and the fact that a large measure of the global imbalance is caused by the United States because of its chronic deficits (fiscal and current account deficits) and by China because of its chronic surpluses (trade surpluses, and surplus in both capital and current accounts), there were calls for the establishment of a G-2 partnership to help work out a global solution to these imbalances (Zheng 2009). The G-2 concept was first proposed by U.S. economist Fred Bergsten advocating a partnership between the United States and China to exercise global economic leadership.

The idea has gained some traction, and champions of the G-2 format in the United States included Robert Zoellick (President of the World Bank) and former U.S. National Security Advisor Zbigniew Brzezinski. The latter had called for an "informal G2 between the two powers that would advance cooperation beyond the frameworks of the G8 and G20" (Lelyveld 2009). Some Chinese intellectuals also see this as a sign that time is ripe for China to assume global leadership.

However, Chinese leaders have remained realistic and pragmatic, taking pains to address misgivings expressed by some countries that the G-2 would monopolize international affairs in the future. Premier Wen Jiabao told reporters at the end of the EU-China Summit in Prague in May that it is baseless and wrong to think that world affairs will be managed by China and the United States. He reiterated China's commitment to multilateralism and a multipolar world (*Xinhua*, 25 May 2009).

Debates continued within both the U.S. and China on the soundness and feasibility of such a framework and the idea of a G-2 remains vague at best. However, there is no doubt that global economic recovery will depend on close cooperation and coordination between the United States and China and Sino-U.S. relations is the most important partnership for global stability.

Need for Rebalancing in Asia — Move from Export-driven Growth to Bolstering Domestic Demand

The current economic crisis exposed the risks of Asian economies' excessive dependence on external demand. The Asian Development Bank (ADB) in its latest report on the global economic crisis warned that export-led growth cannot continue unabated. Countries need to strengthen domestic consumption and President of ADB, Haruhiko Kuroda, urged Asian officials at the annual ADB meeting in Bali to increase spending — on both consumption and investments — to end the dependence on exports.

Rebalancing growth also means altering the composition of aggregate demand in favour of internal demand, matched by changes in the production structure. Many Asian economies because of their favourable accounts surplus and foreign reserves have room for increasing consumer spending. Fiscal resources could be directed to strengthening the social sector protection (health, education, unemployment insurance, pensions). Resilience in domestic consumption and investments in both hard and soft infrastructure can help lead Asia out of the current downturn.

Greater Regional Cooperation in Asia

A concerted global effort is required to effectively address global imbalances. Strengthened regional cooperation in Asia can provide countries with additional resilience. Asia must start to drive its own growth and cut down its dependence on Western markets. Structural decline in demand from advanced economies is to be expected making regional cooperation all the more important. As the ADB report noted, "regional cooperation proved its value during and after the Asian financial crisis and should be strengthened now to prepare for potentially larger shocks ahead" (ADB report 2009).

Greater economic integration within Asia to allow comparative advantages full play among Asian economies will unleash full potential of the region. An earlier analysis by the ADB concludes that regional integration is the way forward for rapid and sustainable growth in Asia. Developing Asia can leverage superior domestic growth rates, accelerate economic diversification and broaden the basis for regional development (Brooks, Roland-Holst and Fan 2005). Another study noted that the creation of an Asian Economic Community can generate gains of US$40 billion to US$176.1 billion depending upon the membership and dept of integration of this community (Mohanty and Pohit 2008).

From Asian Financial Crisis to Global Economic Crisis — ASEAN's Response

The Association of Southeast Asian Nations (ASEAN) was founded on 8 August 1967 at the height of Cold War tensions, and with regional disputes, particularly the "Konfrontasi" unleashed by Indonesia against its smaller neighbours, Singapore and Malaysia, still fresh in the memory. Against this backdrop, the original aim of ASEAN as envisaged by its founding members (Indonesia, Malaysia, the Philippines, Singapore and Thailand) was very modest — to keep the peace in Southeast Asia through respect for each other's sovereignty and adherence to the principle of non-interference. Integration of any kind was never in the game plan. Hence, in the first decade of ASEAN's existence, its priority was to establish an informal and flexible framework in order to accommodate a diversity of opinions and to build confidence.

Being an informal and flexible organization, ASEAN has shown itself generally nimble enough to respond to external challenges in the best possible way. It made its mark as a "diplomatic community" in the 1980s following the Vietnamese invasion of Cambodia in 1978. As new challenges arise in the 1990s, both in the economic and security arena, ASEAN responded with decisions to establish an ASEAN Free Trade Area (AFTA) in 1992 and to launch the first Asia-Pacific forum for security, the ASEAN Regional Forum (ARF) in 1994.

The Asian financial crisis of 1997 took the ASEAN countries by surprise. Coupled with the enlargement of ASEAN to all ten Southeast Asian countries by 1999, ASEAN was faced with unprecedented challenges. ASEAN initial paralysis and disarray in the face of the financial crisis came as a shock, leading later to much soul-searching within the region. The Asian financial crisis revealed the extent of the interdependence between the Southeast Asian region and Northeast Asian region, and at the same time, showed up the weakness of ASEAN in its lack of mechanisms to deal with non-traditional security crisis such as this. It was to catalyze new thinking on region-building in Asia.

ASEAN also embarked on building new regional capacities inspired by the European experiences in response to the increasing economic challenges.

There was also increasing recognition of the need for ASEAN to become a much more integrated and coherent entity if it wants to remain relevant as a grouping and be the driving force behind the various ASEAN plus processes that began to gather momentum after the Asian financial crisis. This culminated into the ambitions of creating an ASEAN Community built on three pillars, the ASEAN Economic Community, the ASEAN Security and Political Community and the ASEAN Socio-Cultural Community. Of the plans in building the three pillars of the community, the most comprehensive has been the action plan towards an ASEAN Economic Community (AEC).

The AEC is in part a response to the global economic landscape that has changed dramatically after the 1997 financial crisis. By 2000, when the ASEAN economies started on its road of recovery, China has moved way ahead in being the most attractive economy in the region, attracting the bulk of FDIs from the developed economies to developing economies. The decade of reforms in India which began in 1991 has also begun to bear fruit. The challenges posed by these two economic giants, China and India, were a wake-up call to ASEAN.

A study commissioned by ASEAN and conducted by McKinsey in 2003 found that middle income ASEAN countries are no longer competitive and the region needs to look for new sources of growth. One key recommendation is for ASEAN to pursue deeper integration in order to take advantage of complementarities between ASEAN economies to achieve economies of scale, industrial efficiency and productivity. Regional production networks need to be revitalized and the nexus between trade and

FDI need to be emphasized. In short, ASEAN need to accelerate its own integration process in order to realize the potential of a market of over 500 million consumers (McKinsey Competitiveness Study Report 2003).

The detailed plan to action to achieve the ASEAN Community in 2020 was spelt out in the Vientiane Action Programme (VAP) adopted in the 2004 Summit in Laos. Of the plans in building the three pillars of the community, the most comprehensive and concrete proposals are in the blueprint for achieving AEC adopted by the leaders in 2007.

According to the AEC Blueprint, the

> AEC is the realization of the end goal of economic integration as espoused in the Vision 2020 which is based on a convergence of interests of ASEAN member countries to deepen and broaden economic integration through existing and new initiatives with clear timeline ... The AEC will establish ASEAN as a single market and production base, making ASEAN more dynamic and competitive with new mechanisms and measures to strengthen the implementation of its existing economic initiatives ... (AEC Blueprint 2007, p. 2).

One could say that the AEC is a logical extension of existing economic initiatives, building on AFTA, AIA and AFAS. The McKinsey study called for bolder and deeper integration within these existing initiatives, and the need to introduce new ones. It particularly focused on the need to create strong institutional mechanisms to see to the implementation of all these initiatives. Specifically, the McKinsey study proposed that given the difficulties of agreeing on cross-sectoral broad and deep liberalization, ASEAN should prioritize a number of sectors to undertake bold liberalization, and in each of these priority sectors, the focus should be on elimination of non-tariff barriers by increasing efficiency of the customs and harmonizing or mutual recognition of standards and regulation; enhance tariff reforms by closer alignment of each member's external tariffs; create a level playing field for capital by eliminating restrictions on cross-border investments within ASEAN and introducing an ASEAN-wide competition policy; and improve regional collaboration in various other areas (Soesastro 2005; McKinsey Competitiveness Study Report 2003).

ASEAN leaders took on board several of these recommendations. Hence in the Action Plan to achieve ASEAN Economic Community, eleven priority sectors for integration were identified (Agro-based products; Electronics; Rubber-based products; Wood-based products; ICT/e-ASEAN; Tourism; Automotive; Fisheries; Textiles and Apparels; Air travel; and Healthcare). The AEC also called for a free and open investment regime and spelt out measures to intensify the implementation of AIA. Liberalization in trade in services and financial cooperation would also be accelerated. To address the problems of implementation associated with AFTA, AIA and AFAS, the AEC reiterated the need to establish an effective system to ensure proper implementation of all economic agreements and expeditious resolution of any disputes through appropriate advisory, consultative and adjudicatory mechanisms (Vientiane Action Programme 2004).

At the 12th ASEAN Summit in January 2006, the ASEAN leaders reaffirmed their commitment to pursuing economic integration by bringing forward the deadline for the establishment of AEC from 2020 to 2015. The AEC Blueprint adopted in November 2007 spelt out in more detail specific action plans and strategic schedule for the achievement of each priority action. "Conceptually, the blueprint brings the constituent parts of the AEC ... and also features a master implementation plan" providing for a review of the AIA and the ASEAN Comprehensive Investment Agreement, renewed focus on completely removing NTBs and initiates a regional discussion on competition policy (Lohman and Kim 2008).

The blueprint is an encouraging demonstration that recognizes the shortcomings of ASEAN thus far, the problems with implementation. ASEAN has never been short of grand declarations and initiatives. However, its implementation record of these various initiatives has thus far been abysmal. The blueprint was organized to show that ASEAN takes the commitments towards economic integration seriously. But then again, the blueprint alone will not lead to economic integration. As Hadi Soesastro pointed out, what ASEAN needs is to find an ASEAN way that is rule-based and governed by stronger institutions. He noted

> there is no point in pursuing an advanced and demanding notion as an AEC without deeper and testable commitment of the member states and stronger institutions or a detailed treaty from the outset. Without endowed ASEAN institutions, without a treaty, without transfer of powers, and without any budget, one should not expect a credible ASEAN Economic Community to emerge (Soesastro 2005).

The decision to establish an ASEAN Charter after almost forty years of ASEAN's existence was seen as a way to address this concern, and transformed ASEAN from a loose, informal organization to a more rules-based organization. The ASEAN Charter is supposed to set the framework and lay the legal foundations for ASEAN to restructure its mechanisms and improve its decision-making process to enhance efficiency and ensure prompt implementation of all ASEAN agreements and decisions.

However, the charter that was unveiled during the 13th Summit in November 2007 drew criticisms from several academics and civil society activists for not going far enough to transform ASEAN. Jusuf Wanandi in his op-ed in *Jakarta Post* expressed disappointment, calling the ASEAN Charter a "mediocre document" and a let-down to the expectations that have been raised. There were high expectations and hope that after "40 years of existence, ASEAN would now face the future with the vision, courage and unity needed to herald the new challenges of the strategic alignments of the 21st Century" (Wanandi 2007). Critics of the charter took issue with the fact that the latter re-emphasized the principle of non-intervention, and continued with a decision-making process that is based on consensus and unanimity.

Overall, the ASEAN Charter did not provide clear evidence of a new ASEAN emerging. Many of the old institutional norms and mechanisms remained, and ASEAN is nowhere near to moving towards any supranational elements. The ASEAN Charter also did not address the implementation deficit that ASEAN suffered because of this lack of institutional mechanisms to ensure or enforce compliance on decisions taken. It reaffirmed a system of coordinating sovereignty rather than pooling sovereignty.

It is thus not surprising that ASEAN was silent in the face of the global economic crisis. In the most recent summit held in Thailand in February 2009, ASEAN could only manage a statement pledging to keep borders open to trade, services and investment and reaffirmed the commitment to achieving an ASEAN Economic Community by 2015. Inaction by ASEAN is also due in part to the domestic political problems of a few key member states as amply reflected by the derailing of the ASEAN-Plus summits and East Asian Summit (EAS) that were to take place in Pattaya in April

2009. The stresses brought about the global economic crisis might accentuate some of these domestic problems.

The lack of a coordinated response from ASEAN put to question the whole façade that ASEAN has tried to maintain for the last ten years as being in the driver's seat behind the various regional architectures. The gaps between rhetoric and reality in ASEAN, between ambitions and ability have unfortunately been widening in the last decade. As long as each individual ASEAN state does not get its house in order, and as long as the ASEAN's non-intervention principles and lowest common denominator approach prevailed, ASEAN would come out short in undertaking clear and concrete commitments to deepen economic integration and to play a leading role in East Asian region-building.

Disappointment with the charter and ASEAN's slow pace of progress has led to increasing voices within Indonesia (the only ASEAN member who is in the G-20) to think beyond ASEAN and stopped treating ASEAN as the cornerstone of Indonesia's foreign policy (Sukma 2008). Another leading intellectual, Jusuf Wanandi, has gone further to suggest a new architecture, a G-8 of East Asia comprising Australia, China, India, Indonesia, Japan, South Korea, Russia and the United States, leaving ASEAN represented by its Secretary-General as an Associate member (Wanandi 2008). Should Indonesia, the largest founding member of ASEAN, decide that ASEAN would no longer be the cornerstone of its foreign policy, there would be significant repercussions on the internal dynamics of ASEAN, and perhaps also on its external engagement of major powers in the region and beyond.

ASEAN+3 Process (China, Japan and South Korea)

ASEAN's progress has been held back by the domestic political problems of some of its member states. Its ability to drive the

ASEAN+3 process is also increasingly in doubt. For ten years since the launch of the APT process in 1997, ASEAN has been on the *de facto* driving seat in part because of the mutual suspicions that Japan and China have towards each other. ASEAN's role was crucial and the ASEAN+3 process an important platform for the Northeast Asian economies to continue to meet each other even at one point when relations between China and Japan hit a new low in 2004–05.

The APT process has made significant progress particularly in the area of monetary cooperation. Having experienced the Asian financial crisis, the thirteen East and Southeast Asian countries agreed in 2000 to establish a currency swap arrangement known as the Chiang Mai Initiative (CMI) to help each other in the eventuality of another currency crisis. Consisting of a series of bilateral swap agreements, an agreement to multilateralize the swap agreement was reached in 2005. A regional surveillance mechanism called the Economic Review and Policy Dialogue (ERPD) was also put in place. It was hoped that the ERPD would "evolve to the point of providing information and analysis that would permit the identification of vulnerabilities among members and provide a foundation for regionally defined conditionality in the event that the BSAs were called upon (Henning 2009).

In the midst of the current economic crisis, senior officials of the ASEAN+3 countries and their central banks have met three times between February 2009 to May 2009 and finally agreed to the establishment of a fund worth US$120 billion. Members of the CMI can tap on this regional pool of foreign exchange reserves "to better fend off a financial crisis" (Rathus 2009). China and Japan each contributed 32 per cent to the fund, South Korea, 16 per cent and the rest of the 20 per cent from the ASEAN economies. However, differences remained with regards to issues over economic surveillance and where to establish the CMI Secretariat.

What has been striking in the latest development in the APT process with regards to the CMI is the fact that China, Japan and Korea have been much more proactive in expediting the process of multilateralization of the CMI. These three countries organized their first self-standing trilateral summit in Fukuoka on 13 December 2008 when the ASEAN Summit and its attendant APT Summit and East Asia Summit has to be postponed because of the political crisis in Thailand, the Chair of ASEAN for 2008–09. The lack of coherence in ASEAN and the fact that ASEAN has let domestic issues of one member state held the regional processes hostage came at the most awkward time when intense regional efforts are required to confront the challenges posed by the global economic crisis. It also called into question ASEAN's continued validity for occupying the driver's seat of the various regional processes.

ASEAN and the West

Efforts in the past few years to bring up EU-ASEAN relations have borne some results. The EU has since 2003 adopted a much more pragmatic approach in its relations with ASEAN after it revealed its new strategy paper toward the Southeast Asian region. Entitled "A New Partnership with Southeast Asia", this paper called for a multi-track approach to circumvent the thorny issue of Myanmar. Relations with some countries within ASEAN can move faster through bilateral cooperation agreements. The agreements can also be tailored to meet the different needs of the ASEAN countries, with focus on development cooperation to the less prosperous countries, and on trade, investments, research cooperation, political dialogue with the more developed countries.

In the document the European Commission noted that the desire to revitalize the EU's relations with ASEAN is built on the assumption that the countries of Europe and Southeast Asia share many common features and values… (including) a deep respect for cultural, religious and linguistic diversity, and a commitment to regional integration. There is also the increasing realization that many problems such as terrorism, environmental degradation, diseases, organized crimes are truly global in their nature, and can only be addressed effectively through international cooperation (Communication from the Commission, 9 July 2003, p. 1).

There are strong economic reasons for deepening ASEAN-EU engagement. In 2007, the EU is ASEAN's second largest trading partner while ASEAN is the EU's fifth largest trading partner. The EU is also the biggest source of FDI in ASEAN. ASEAN's promise to build an AEC by 2015 and talk of transforming itself into a more rule-based organization on its 40th anniversary offered the EU a good reason for stepping up engagement with ASEAN. Hence, in 2007, negotiations were launched for an EU-ASEAN FTA.

However, ASEAN now increasingly risked being sidelined. The lack of progress in achieving greater economic integration dilutes ASEAN's attractiveness as a potential market of 550 million consumers. As Razeen Sally put it, "there will be no true AEC — an integrated market for goods, services, investment and skilled labour — by 2015. Beyond supply-chain integration in a few sectors (mainly in the ICT), ASEAN has no single market" (Sally 2009). The EU's FTA negotiations with ASEAN has also been stuck. Efforts to bring up EU-ASEAN relations has borne some results but the crisis if prolonged is likely to take the EU's attention away, and the temptation toward protectionism cannot be ruled out.

ASEAN has often "accused" the United States of benign neglect of the region. Indeed there is widespread perception that America's commitment to the region is declining. The Bush administration's narrow focus on terrorism as the key agenda in

U.S. relations with Southeast Asia has also irked several of the ASEAN states. What ASEAN wanted was a comprehensive dialogue with the United States, and for it not only to deal bilaterally with the various ASEAN countries but to also treat Southeast Asia as a community and take ASEAN seriously.

According to the Asian Foundation report, the U.S.-ASEAN economic relationship is substantial, growing and mutually beneficial. The cumulative stock of American investments in Southeast Asia is about US$100 billion which is higher than that in China or India. Despite this, and even with the change of the U.S. Government, there is the perception that a negative attitude towards ASEAN persists as a number of U.S. officials regard ASEAN as a talkshop and an ineffectual regional organization. The United States continues to prefer dealing bilaterally with each ASEAN member state (Koh 2008).

In the past few years, ASEAN's partnership with the United States is often contrasted with that of China. In order to raise U.S. interest in ASEAN, China's charm offensive and gains in the region is often highlighted to get the U.S. attention on the strategic importance of the region to the United States. In the face of the current global crisis, this "ploy" may no longer work as the United States and China need to work hand in hand to rebalance the global economy. ASEAN's silence and lack of response to the economic crisis may well confirm to the Americans the weakness of ASEAN.

Conclusion

The real impact of the global economic crisis has not been fully played out within ASEAN and the extent of its "damage" to ASEAN is still not fully appreciated. Several key ASEAN players are caught in its own domestic political troubles and not sufficient attention has been paid to articulate a coordinated response and a vision of the way forward in coping with the global crisis. No one expects ASEAN to lead the economic recovery, but the relative inaction may mean that ASEAN would lose its driver's seat in East Asia. China will probably become increasing assertive in the region. The Northeast Asian partners of ASEAN were instrumental in multilateralization of the CMI and launching the US$120 billion fund as an insurance against further shocks.

The preliminary prognosis for ASEAN is that current global economic crisis will alter significantly the region's dynamics resulting in less room for ASEAN's manoeuvrability. Strategic dialogue with its Northeast Asian neighbours, particularly China, will increase in importance while dialogue with its Western partners will decline due in part also to the Western preoccupation with their own recovery and internal processes. ASEAN's lack of real integration and failure to establish a credible ASEAN Economic Community by 2015 would further sideline ASEAN in the overall regional landscape.

References

ADB Report. "The Global Economic Crisis: Challenges for Developing Asia and ADB's Response", April 2009 (Download from Asian Development Bank's website).

Altman, Roger C. "The Great Crash 2008: A Geopolitical Setback for the West". *Foreign Affairs*, January/February 2009.

"Asian Growth to Slow Sharply in 2009, IMF Says". *IMF Survey Online*, 24 November 2008. <www.imf.org/external/pubs/ft/survey/so/2008/CAR112408A.htm>.

Bezlova, Antoaneta. "China Pulling Southeast Asia into its Orbit". Global Geopolitics Net Sites, 1 May 2009. <http://globalgeopolitics.net/wordpress/2009/05/01/politics-china-pulling-southeast-asia-into-its-orbit> (accessed 4 June 2009).

"Crisis Deals Sharp Blow to Asian Growth". *IMF Survey Online*, 6 May 2009. <www.imf.org/external/pubs/ft/survey/so/2009/car050509a. htm>.

Henning, C. Randall. "The Future of the Chiang Mai Initiative: An Asian Monetary Fund? Peterson Institute for International Economics". Policy Brief No. PB09-5, February 2009.

Hill, Hal. "Political Realignment in Southeast Asia". *Far Eastern Economic Review*, April 2009. <http://feer.com/essays/2009/april/political-realignment-in-southeast-asia> (accessed 4 June 2009).

Koh, Tommy. "The United States and Southeast Asia". Asia Foundation Report on America's Role in Asia, 2008, pp. 35–54.

Lelyaveld, Michael. "US-China G2 Plan Sparks Debate". <www.rfa.org/english/energy_watch/us-china-g2-05042009161703.htm>.

Lohman, Walter and Anthony Kim. "Enabling ASEAN's Economic Vision". Backgrounder No. 2101, 29 January 2009. Published by the Heritage Foundation.

Lopez, Gregory. "ASEAN's Response to the Global Crisis". <www.igloo.org/eastasiaintegration/aseanresp>.

McKinsey. Competitiveness Study Report, 2003.

Moisi, Dominique. "A Global Downturn in the Power of the West". *Straits Times*, 8 October 2008.

Parello-Plesner, Jonas. "The G-2: No Good for China and for World Governance". <www.eastasiaforum.org/2009.05/23/the-g-2-no-good-for-china-and-for-world-governance>.

Rathus, Joel. "The Chiang Mai Initiative: China, Japan and Financial Regionalism". <www.eastasiaforum.org/2009/05/11/the-chiang-mai-initiative-china-japan-and-financial-regionalism>.

Sally, Razeen. "ASEAN Charteritis". <www.eastasiaforum.org/2009/03/13/asean-charteritis>.

Soesastro, Hadi. "Accelerating ASEAN Economic Integration: Moving Beyond AFTA". Economics Working Paper Series, March 2005.

Sukma, Rizal. "ASEAN Members should Stop having Themselves on".

<www.eastasiaforum.org/2008/12/02/asean-members-should-stop-having-themselves-on>.

Wanandi, Jusuf. "ASEAN Charter: Does a Mediocre Document really Matter?". *Jakarta Post*, 26 November 2007.

———. "The ASEAN Charter and Remodelling Regional Architecture". <www.eastasiaforum.org/2008/11/09/the-asean-charter-and-remodeling-regional-architecture>.

Zheng, Yongnian. "Sino-American Relations: The G20 and the Future G2?". EAI Background Brief No. 449, 28 April 2009.

Official Documents (available on ASEAN Secretariat website at <www.aseansec.org>).

ASEAN Charter.

ASEAN Economic Community Blueprint.

Recommendations of the High Level Task Force on ASEAN Economic Integration.

Vientiane Action Programme.

Yeo Lay Hwee is the Director of the European Union Centre. She is also a Senior Research Fellow at Singapore Institute of International Affairs.

3
ASEAN'S RESPONSE MECHANISMS FOR LABOUR AND SOCIAL PROTECTION: CHALLENGES IN CREATING CRISIS-RESILIENT ECONOMIES[1]

Kazutoshi Chatani and Kee Beom Kim

The Economic and Social Impacts of the Global Crisis in ASEAN[2]

Economic Impact and Transmission Mechanisms

While many ASEAN member countries only saw moderate deceleration in economic growth in 2008, as the crisis intensified and demand began to sharply slow in the United States, the European Union and Japan, a substantial decline in economic activity took place in many of these countries from late 2008 and 2009. Current IMF forecasts indicate that economic growth in the Asia region as a whole will drop to 1.4 per cent this year while the ASEAN-5 countries combined may see no growth in 2009.[3]

There are a number of ways in which the current crisis is being transmitted to ASEAN economies. Understanding the specific mechanisms through which industries and economies are being affected is essential for assessing the likely labour market impact and for designing appropriate policies to mitigate the adverse effects.

Exports have played a major role in ASEAN's strong growth performance in past decades, with many ASEAN economies highly reliant on exports to earn foreign currency and fuel domestic development. Heading into the crisis, manufacturing exports comprised more than 140 per cent of GDP in Singapore, nearly 70 per cent in Malaysia, more than 40 per cent in Cambodia and Thailand and more than 30 per cent in the Philippines and Vietnam. On the other hand, manufacturing exports make up only around 11 per cent in Indonesia.[4] As consumers in developed economies abruptly cut back on spending in 2008 and the beginning of 2009, demand for ASEAN's exports have fallen sharply. The January 2009 export data for Malaysia and the Philippines indicated an astounding year-on-year drop of more than 34 per cent and 41 per cent, respectively.[5] Accordingly, many firms in the ASEAN region have sharply cut production, with an unmistakable rise in factory closures.

Foreign direct investment (FDI) has also been an important contributor to growth in many ASEAN economies — allowing them to move up the value chain through increased access to both capital and more advanced technologies. As a share of gross fixed capital formation, FDI comprises some 60 per cent in Singapore, 52 per cent in Cambodia and 25 per cent in Vietnam. FDI also accounts for a large share of capital formation in Malaysia, Pakistan, Thailand and the Philippines. In 2008, growth in FDI turned negative in several Asian countries, including Singapore, Thailand and Indonesia.[6] Overall, current estimates are that total FDI to developing countries will shrink by more than 30 per cent in 2009, and while Asia may continue to outperform other developing regions with regard to attracting FDI, the chance is slim that the region can avoid a decline in foreign investment.[7] In

Cambodia, for example, FDI in 2009 is forecast to contract to US$390 million, about half the amount in 2008.[8]

As migrant workers' incomes are at risk in the current economic downturn, so too are remittances, which represent a vital source of income and foreign exchange for many ASEAN economies, and in particular for poor households. Remittances comprise between 7–12 per cent of GDP in the Philippines and Vietnam. Remittance flows to developing economies began to slow in the third quarter of 2008 and the World Bank now forecasts an overall fall in remittances to these economies in 2009 of approximately 5 per cent.[9] In addition to remittances, official aid flows are likely to be affected by tighter budgets in advanced economies. This is likely to add pressure in the region's least developed countries to government budget items directed toward economic development and poverty reduction.

Labour Market Impact

While the impact of the crisis on ASEAN's labour market will differ by country, a few common patterns and particularly vulnerable groups are emerging from the available information to date. The first is of these patterns is growing job losses. Thousands of workers in key export industries in the region have been retrenched. In Malaysia, the number of retrenched workers totalled 12,600 in the first quarter of 2009.[10] While the absolute number of retrenched workers may be small, the number is nearly a four-fold increase from the average quarterly number of retrenched workers in 2008 of 3,460. More than three-fourths of the retrenched workers in the first quarter of 2009 were in manufacturing.

In Indonesia, the Ministry of Manpower and Transmigration reported that job reductions exceeded 51,000 workers while the Indonesian Employers' Association (APINDO) reported 237,000 lay-offs between October 2008 and March 2009, with the textile and garments sector accounting for the bulk of those retrenchments, followed by palm oil plantations, automotive and spare parts, construction and footwear.[11] In Cambodia, employment in the garment sector contracted by 15 per cent between September 2008 and February 2009.[12] In Thailand, the number of persons on unemployment insurance rose by 17.2 per cent in January 2009 alone, after rising by 38.3 per cent in 2008 compared to the previous year.[13]

While the direct impact in terms of cutting existing jobs can be approximated, what is more difficult to measure is how many more jobs would have been created in the absence of the financial crisis. Employment growth of 7.9 million jobs from 2006 to 2007 in ASEAN offers a perspective in this regard. In other words, the impact of the global crisis may imply substantial "opportunity" costs.[14] The implications are all the more relevant for countries with high population growth rates. Some of these countries already faced serious youth employment challenges that are further aggravated by the global crisis.

In situations of high levels of poverty and inadequate social safety nets, workers who have lost their jobs are left with few alternatives except to turn to lower productivity and informal economic activities. One useful indicator in this regard is the number and share of workers in vulnerable employment, which is defined as the sum of own-account workers and unpaid family workers. Many workers in these types of employment status in developing economies do not enjoy social protection in case of job loss, personal or family illnesses or other difficulties; they are less likely than formal wage employees to receive an adequate income and to have their fundamental labour rights respected. Women comprise a disproportionately large share in vulnerable employment throughout the region.

A larger impact than job losses in ASEAN and Asia more generally is the shift to informal and vulnerable employment, including the rural economy. Recent official data in Indonesia and Thailand corroborate this trend. In Indonesia, the number of employees expanded by 1.4 per cent between February 2008 and February 2009 but occupations considered more vulnerable outpaced the growth in wage employment during the same period. In particular, the number of casual workers outside agriculture increased by around 7.3 per cent during the period. In Thailand, the fourth quarter 2008 figures indicate that the number of wage employees contracted by more than 100,000 or by 0.6 per cent, while the number of own-account and contributing family workers combined increased by an astounding 800,000 compared to the previous year.

As many workers in vulnerable employment are more likely to be in the lower end of the income spectrum, trends in vulnerable employment are linked with trends in working poverty. A great deal of uncertainty remains as to how the current crisis will affect overall levels of poverty and working poverty in the Asia region. However, a substantial impact will likely be felt by the workers and households who have risen just barely above the poverty line in recent years due to new formal employment opportunities and are now vulnerable to falling back into poverty as a result of the crisis. More than 52 million workers are estimated to be living just 10 per cent above the extreme US$1.25 poverty line, while more than 140 million living just 20 per cent above the extreme poverty line.[15]

Recommended Labour Market Responses to the Global Crisis

Greater focus on employment and social protection policies would enhance the resilience of economies of ASEAN member countries to the crisis as well as accelerate the recovery process. Since the current global financial and economic crisis is characterized by a steep fall in global aggregate demand, it is not an option in the short run for any country to export its way out of the crisis. Stimulating domestic economic activities and supporting domestic aggregate demand through employment and social protection is a viable policy direction, which would also serve to induce a gradual recovery of global trade. Coherent employment and enterprise policies at the global, regional and the national level, renewed commitment of each nation to a basic floor of social protection, upholding fundamental principles and rights at work and international labour standards are required for sustained and accelerated economic, employment and social recovery. It must be borne in mind that the recovery in the labour market typically lags the economic recovery by four to five years and hence the need for continued vigilance of the labour market even after output recovery. The continuous attention of policy-makers is required to support vulnerable groups in the labour market as well as monitoring the trends in quantity and the quality of employment.

In particular, the following responses may be considered:

Support Small and Medium-sized Enterprises (SMEs)

A large number of workers are employed in small and medium-sized enterprises (SMEs) across ASEAN member countries and their employment is at stake since many SMEs are threatened by the declining global demand for their products and services, directly or indirectly through intertwined supply chains. In addition to falling sales, the ailing financial market severely engenders the survival of otherwise sound businesses. In addition, financial institutions perceive higher risks of non-performing loans and are reluctant in granting new or additional loans. Central banks in the region have cut interest rates to support the industry; however, SMEs are often not in a position to benefit from these initiatives compared to their larger counterparts. Restoring credit and the normal function of financial markets are of high priority in safeguarding SMEs, the backbone of employment. In the meanwhile, the governments in the region must give due policy attention to alleviating cash-flow problems that confront SMEs. Measures to this end *inter alia* include providing credit guarantees by the government or public banks, relaxing collateral requirements, speeding up loan appraisals, and creating venture capital funds or new types of financial instruments for SMEs. Allowing access to competitive credit lines would effectively prevent unnecessary lay-offs and wage cuts and support the economy in a recovery.

Social Dialogue and Collective Bargaining as a Tool to Cushion the Impact of the Crisis on Workers

Social dialogue can play a vital role in mitigating the labour market and social impact of the crisis on workers and their family members as well as facilitating adjustment at the company level. Social partners can join forces and flexibly arrange acceptable alternative solutions to lay-offs. Safeguarding existing jobs, for example, prevents a loss of firm-specific skills while reducing firing costs as well as (re)hiring and (re)training costs when the economy starts picking up. Lay-offs should be considered as a last resort and alternative solutions to lay-offs include *inter alia*: working hour reduction, work sharing, (re)training and wage moderation. Some enterprises consider the period of slack production as an opportunity to upgrade workers' skills and productivity. The government may wish to assist with alternative arrangements to lay-offs by offering targeted reductions in social security

Box 3.1

A New Consensus — Sustainable Enterprises

In 2007, the tripartite constituents at the International Labour Conference discussed the issue of sustainable enterprises and concluded that: "A well-functioning financial system provides the lubricant for a growing and dynamic private sector. Making it easier for small and medium-sized enterprises, including cooperatives and start-ups, to access financing, for example credit, leasing, venture capital funds or similar or new types of instruments, creates appropriate conditions for a more inclusive process of enterprise development. Financial institutions, particularly multilateral and international ones, should be encouraged to include decent work in their lending practices." These conclusions are all the more relevant in the context of the global crisis.

For further information, see ILO, Conclusions Concerning the Promotion of Sustainable Enterprises (Geneva 2007).

contributions and/or supporting training to upgrade the skills of at-risk workers.

In addition to facilitating the identification of solutions to the challenges posed by the global crisis, social dialogue provides the basis for sustainable socioeconomic development. For example, the ILO Declaration on Social Justice for a Fair Globalization (2008) notes that "promoting social dialogue and tripartism are most appropriate methods for:

• Applying Decent Work strategic objectives in national circumstances;

- Translating economic development into social progress;
- Building consensus on employment and labour policies; and
- Making labour law and institutions effective".

Policies Targeted at Vulnerable Groups

Some groups of workers are particularly vulnerable to the economic slowdown, requiring the special attention of policy-makers. For example, the youth employment situation is likely to deteriorate since large numbers of school leavers will join the labour force despite the crisis. The scarcity of employment opportunities due to the crisis will make their job search efforts even more strenuous.

Women form another vulnerable group in the labour market. Owing to the high concentration of working women in export sectors, women are significantly affected by the crisis. In addition, women are likely to shoulder the intensified double burden of family care and income generating activities, in part because of reduced men's take-home wages and the lack of formal care systems. For these reasons, national policy responses must take the gender dimensions into account. Enhancing equal access to public works to both women and men can be achieved, for example, by including social services and environment protection components in such schemes.

Migrant workers and their families are also particularly vulnerable in times of crisis. Migrant workers, especially undocumented ones, may be the subject of discrimination and exploitation. Governments should ensure the full application of the principle of equal treatment and non-discrimination for migrant workers. Countries experiencing large-scale return migration may need to devise targeted employment policies and other mechanisms that lend help to repatriated overseas migrant workers.

Expanding and Enhancing Social Protection

As noted earlier, the economic crisis is leading to job losses in the formal sector and an expansion in the informal economy. Furthermore, an increased labour supply in the informal economy can lead to deterioration in the working conditions of informal workers, increasing and deepening poverty as a consequence. The expansion and implementation of social protection programmes in the informal economy are thus of critical need.

Well-designed and targeted employment guarantee programmes can be a cost-effective policy tool and has a proven track record in Argentina and Indonesia. India's National Rural Employment Guarantee Act (NREGA) is of particular interest as the programme addresses employment creation, rural development, social protection and poverty alleviation simultaneously. The programme targets poor informal workers in rural areas and guarantees 100 days of work, with 33 per cent of employment reserved for women. NREGA created about 1.4 billion person days of work in 2007–08, of which about 42 for women at the cost was about 0.5 per cent of the GDP. This type of employment policy is particularly effective in times of crisis as it provides the poor and with a minimum income security, mitigating the impoverishing effect of the global economic slowdown.

Related to employment guarantee schemes, employment-intensive approaches to infrastructure investment can support employment creation, local economic development and poverty alleviation. These approaches are also known as local resource-based (LRB) approaches given the optimum and flexible use of locally available workforce, materials, skills and capacities.

Employment-intensive (or LRB) approaches are effective in mitigating the adverse impact of the crisis on a labour market because of their high capacity in absorbing labour. Many countries in the region including Indonesia, the Philippines and Cambodia have benefited from these approaches to infrastructure development.

Among various social assistance programmes, there is evidence from impact evaluations that conditional cash transfer schemes bring real benefits to poor households in terms of reducing poverty, increasing investment in child schooling and healthcare.[16] Furthermore, they have in general resulted in reductions in child labour and no significant negative impacts on the labour market participation of adults.[17] Indonesia for example is currently implementing a conditional cash transfer scheme — The Hopeful Family Programme. School subsidies and scholarships are other examples of effective social policy interventions, since they help keep children in school and reduce the incidence of child labour. These programmes thus lead to the double dividend of providing effective social protection the short term and reducing the inter-generational poverty traps in the longer term. It must be noted however, that the successful implementation of all these programmes is contingent upon the administrative capacity of implementing agencies and partners, which raises the need to strengthen labour market institutions.

In the framework of its Campaign for the Extension of Social Security to All and as part of its constitutional mandate, the ILO is promoting a basic and modest set of essential social transfers that could ensure:

- Universal access to essential health services for all residents;
- Income security for all children through child benefits;

- Modest income support for the poor in active age combined with employment guarantees through public works programmes; and
- Income security through basic tax-financed pensions for the old, the disabled and those who have lost the main breadwinner in a family.

Such a set of minimum guarantees is affordable for most countries. An ILO costing study of twelve developing countries indicates that the initial gross annual cost of the overall basic social protection package (excluding access to basic health care that to some extent is financed already) is projected to be in the range of 2.3 to 5.5 per cent of GDP.[18] Individual elements appear even more affordable. The annual cost of providing universal basic old-age and disability pensions, for example, is estimated at between 0.6 and 1.5 per cent of GDP in the countries considered. Some low-income countries may require the support of the international donor community for the transition period that these countries increase domestic resources or reallocate existing resources.

Current Social Protection in ASEAN Countries[19]

Social protection schemes in ASEAN member countries are in general at an early stage of development. While public sector employees in all ASEAN member countries except Cambodia enjoy social insurance, the general public is not necessarily covered by similar social insurance. In addition, the vast majority of informal workers are excluded from existing social protection. Brunei Darussalam is the only country among ASEAN member countries that has a universal pension. In many cases, social protection programmes are managed by various organizations and remain fragmented. At the regional level, the ASEAN member

---

Box 3.2
A Global Jobs Pact

The Global Jobs Pact is a policy package, proposed by the ILO and agreed to by the ILO's tripartite constituency, which aims to alleviate the adverse impact of the global financial crisis on workers and companies in all sectors including the rural and informal economy. It acts as a catalyst for productive and sustainable recovery since it leverages economic stimulus packages and other relevant national policies to address employment and labour market issues and to promote social protection and respect for workers' rights. Social dialogue is a key consensus-building tool indispensable to the pact.

For further information, see: ILO, Recovering from the Crisis: A Global Jobs Pact (Geneva 2009).

---

countries regularly exchange information on social protection; however, formulating regional coherent policies or strategies to strengthen social protection is a future task. Table 3.1 summarizes various schemes of social protection in place in ASEAN member countries.

Poverty and healthcare costs can constitute a vicious circle of poverty: individuals and their families are pushed into poverty by healthcare costs in the absence of social insurance or universal healthcare. Among the ASEAN member states, Brunei, Malaysia, Thailand and the Philippines have been successful in achieving (quasi) universal health insurance coverage or a universal healthcare system, while social health protection is still a challenge for the poor and informal economy workers in some ASEAN

TABLE 3.1

Social Protection Schemes in ASEAN Member States

	Brunei	Cambodia	Indonesia	Laos	Malaysia	Myanmar	Philippines	Singapore	Thailand	Vietnam
Old age	P/U		P	S	P		S	P	S	S
Invalidity	P/U		P	S	S/P		S	P	S	S
Survivors	P		P	S	S/P		S	P	S	S
Medical care	U		S	S	U	S	S	P/A	U/S	S
Sickness	E	E	E	S	E		S	E	S	S
Maternity	E	E	E	S	E		S	E	S	S
Work injury	E	S	S	S	S/E	S	S	E	S	S

Note: S: social insurance, P: provident fund, U: universal, E: employer liability, A: social assistance.

Source: Hiroshi Yamabana, "Overview of Social Protection Scheme in Asia Pacific Countries", a presentation delivered at Kuala Lumpur on 19 August 2008.

member countries. Healthcare costs in Southeast Asia are largely financed by out-of-pocket spending and social health insurance plays a limited role. The share of tax-based healthcare funding is low relative to other regions (see Figure 3.1). There is thus a need for health financing in the region to gradually shift from out-of-pocket spending to social insurance and universal coverage based on taxation in order to expand healthcare coverage.

Unemployment insurance schemes are still limited for most countries in ASEAN member countries. Thailand implemented unemployment insurance in 2004 and Vietnam followed in 2009. Other countries still rely on severance payments for providing income security in case of job loss. Severance payments, however,

FIGURE 3.1
Composition of Health Spending — 2001
(Data estimated using average annual
exchange rate — Timor Leste not included)

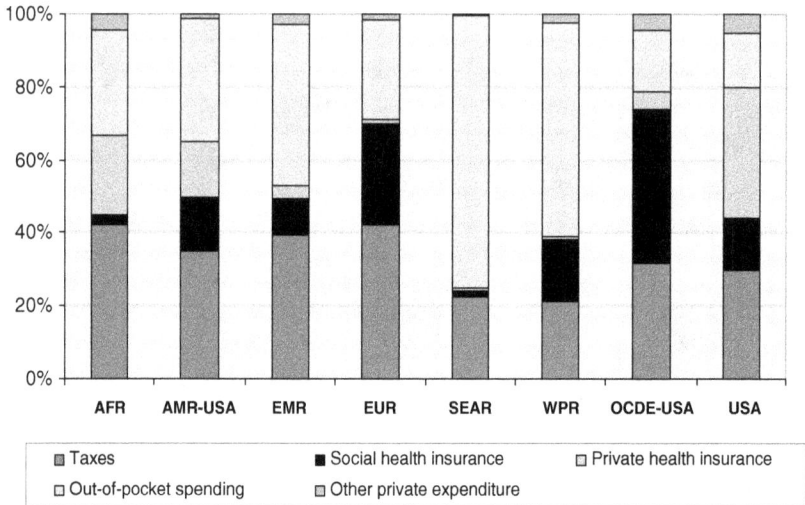

Note: AFR: Africa, AMR: Americas, EMR: East Mediterranean, EUR: Europe, SEAR: Southeast Asia, WPR: Western Pacific.
Source: NHA Unit, EIP/FER/RER, World Health Organization.

may fail to provide sufficient income security especially when companies become insolvent. Furthermore, severance payments are seldom linked with active labour market policies such as vocational training and employment placement services.

Moving Forward

At the summit meeting in January 2007, the ASEAN leaders committed themselves to accelerating integration between member countries, with the ultimate aim of establishing an ASEAN Community by 2015. They envisaged that greater integration within the region will help to narrow the gaps in development between member countries and allow each to maximize their productivity, competitiveness and individual development potential. At the same time, all stand to benefit from the many advantages that a large, single market would offer. Greater integration would create a protective environment, offering security, stability, shared prosperity and social progress.

Nonetheless, as highlighted in earlier sections, a crucial challenge to achieving greater integration entails strengthening the social dimension of integration. The 1997–98 Asian financial crisis served to highlight that without social dimension policies, including effective labour market and social protection policies, irreversible losses in human capital occur, undermining sustainable development and social progress.

In recognition, the ASEAN Socio-Cultural Community Blueprint contains elements on strengthening social protection. In that blueprint, "ASEAN is committed to enhancing the well-being and the livelihood of the peoples of ASEAN through alleviating poverty, ensuring social welfare and protection, building a safe, secure and drug free environment, enhancing disaster resilience and addressing health development concerns." Furthermore, the blueprint seeks to "ensure that all ASEAN peoples are provided with social welfare and protection from the possible negative impacts of globalization and integration by improving the quality, coverage and sustainability of social protection and increasing the capacity of social risk management".

In light of the above commitments, the time has come to strengthen the social dimension of regional integration through improved access to basic healthcare, protection for children, the elderly and people with disabilities, social assistance for people who are poor or unemployed and other features that vary according to country needs and stages of development. Building such a "social floor" is crucial in times of crisis but also in coping with adjustment that accompany dynamic societies and economies. Such a floor is vital in ensuring security, and guaranteeing equal opportunities for everyone to participate and benefit from the process of integration. Success in this regard is crucial to the longer-term viability of economic integration and the underlying social fabric. The current crisis is an opportunity to realize the long-pending agenda of extending basis social protection to cover all women and men. The cost of a basic social floor can be made affordable in ASEAN member countries.

In the context of the crisis, social assistance programmes such as targeted cash transfers and employment programmes are generally regarded as the most effective way for governments to support the purchasing power of vulnerable households. Employment programmes can create much-needed employment opportunities in local public works projects and if cash transfers are linked to a certain conditions, such as low income, occupation or location, or to a mandated behaviour, such as sending children to school and not to work or attending health clinics, they can lead to double dividends for policy-makers. While providing effective social safety nets in the short term, such transfer programmes can help reduce inter-generational poverty traps in the longer term.

Social protection, rather than a cost, is a key investment in human capital which in turn is a critical driver of competitiveness. Until now, many low- and medium-income ASEAN countries have pursued a growth strategy based on high savings rates, fixed investment, abundant labour supplies and export promotion. However, this formula is becoming less and less appropriate as competition from China, India and other emerging economies is mounting and labour force growth in some countries is slowing down. Moreover, this approach to growth is unsustainable in the long term because it tends to neglect the intangible assets of economic competitiveness, such as innovation and creativity.[20] As these countries begin to focus on developing more efficient production processes and improving product quality, competitiveness becomes increasingly driven by the quality of the workforce and by the ways in which human resources are managed at the workplace. For ASEAN countries moving into, or already at, a higher stage of development, the only way to sustain economic growth and social development is to compete through innovation in products, processes and technologies, using well-educated workers and progressive workplace practices. A social floor provides the reassurance for innovation, human capital deepening and the foundation for productivity growth.

In close cooperation with employers' and workers' organizations, governments can review how the basic components of their social security system meet the needs of their economic and social development objectives in the context of the crisis but also the rapidly changing economic, demographic and social circumstances. Asides from immediate crisis measures, the broader social protection system in ASEAN member countries can be strengthened incrementally according to each country's realities and priorities. This could empower millions to move out of poverty and further ahead in life. Furthermore, ASEAN member countries should collectively seek to establish mechanisms for learning and sharing of information on strengthening social protection and, in particular, extending it to the informal economy.

The involvement of the tripartite partners — governments, employers and workers — is particularly important in undertaking the needed social protection reforms. Importantly, all three share the common fundamental goal of achieving sustainable growth and social progress. To realize this goal, businesses will require productivity growth and upward mobility in the value chain to ensure long-term competitiveness; and workers will require access to decent work, meaningul opportunities through productive employment creation, empowerment through the recognition of their fundamental rights, security through social protection, and an effective voice through democratic institutions and social dialogue. In addition to mobilizing support for needed reforms and ensuring their effective implementation and monitoring, good mechanisms for social dialogue, combined with mutual understanding between government, businesses and workers, can foster cooperation and innovation, allowing them to find negotiated solutions in dynamic labour markets. This could, in turn, support not only an environment conducive to investment and growth; it could also become a unique source of the region's competitiveness in the years to come.

In addition to collaboration among ASEAN member countries, greater coordination and collaboration at other levels are required for a coherent response to the crisis and in building effective social protection systems. In this regard, building on the ILO/ASEAN *Cooperation Agreement* and past collaboration with ASEAN member countries in the area of social protection as well as other interconnected areas, the ILO is continuing to support ASEAN in extending the effectiveness and coverage of social protection and in addressing the current economic crisis, with the Decent Work Agenda and the Asian Decent Work Decade providing the framework.

Notes

1. At the roundtable, this paper was presented by Peter Van Rooij, Deputy Director, International Labour Organization, Jakarta and ASEAN Liaison, Indonesia.

2.   This section draws upon P. Huynh, S. Kapsos, K.B. Kim, and
     G. Sziraczki, "Impacts of the Current Global Economic Crisis on
     Asia's Labour Market", Asian Development Bank Institute Working
     Paper (ADBI, forthcoming).
3.   IMF, *World Economic Outlook: Crisis and Recovery*, April 2009.
     ASEAN-5 includes Indonesia, Malaysia, the Philippines, Thailand
     and Vietnam.
4.   World Trade Organization, Statistics Database, October 2008.
5.   World Bank, *East Asia and Pacific Update: Battling the Forces of
     Global Recession*, April 2009 (World Trade Organization: Statistics
     Database, October 2008).
6.   United Nations Conference on Trade and Development (UNCTAD),
     "Global Foreign Direct Investment Now in Decline — and Estimated
     to have Fallen during 2008", UNCTAD/PRESS/PR/2009/001.rev1,
     19 January 2009.
7.   Patricia Lui, "Emerging Markets Face $180 Billion Investment
     Decline", *Bloomberg*, 21 January 2009.
8.   World Bank, *East Asia and Pacific Update: Battling the Forces of
     Global Recession*, April 2009.
9.   Dilip Ratha and Sanket Mohapatra, *Revised Outlook for Remittance
     Flows 2009–2011: Remittances expected to fall by 5 to 8 per cent
     in 2009*, Migration and Development Brief No. 9 (Washington,
     D.C.: World Bank, March 2009).
10. Malaysia Ministry of Human Resources. From the number of total
     lay-offs reported between 1 October 2008 and 14 May 2009, it
     appears that around 75 per cent of retrenchments are permanent,
     while 25 per cent of retrenchments took place under voluntary
     separation schemes.
11. "This Year's Unemployment Target is 8 per cent", *Tempo Interactive*,
     13 May 2009; "Total Workers Laid off Reach over 200,000: Apindo",
     Jakarta Post, 12 March 2009.
12. H. Jalilian et al., "Global Financial Crisis Discussion Series Paper 4:
     Cambodia" (London: ODI, 2009).
13. Thailand Office of National Economic and Social Development

Board, "Economic Outlook: Thai Economic Performance in Q4 and Outlook for 2009", 23 February 2009.

14. ILO, *Labour and Social Trends in ASEAN 2008*, 2008.

15. ILO, *Trends Econometric Models*, December 2008.

16. A. Fiszbein and N. Schady, *Conditional Cash Transfers: Reducing Present and Future Poverty* (Washington: World Bank, 2009).

17. Ibid.

18. ILO, *Can Low-income Countries Afford Basic Social Security* (Geneva, 2008).

19. This section draws from Fifi Anggraini Arif, "Social Protection and Social Pension in ASEAN Region: Strengthening Regional Cooperation", a presentation delivered at the South East Asia Social Pension Meeting on 22 January 2009, Chiang Mai, Thailand and Hiroshi Yamabana, "Overview of Social Protection Scheme in Asia Pacific Countries", a presentation delivered at Kuala Lumpur on 19 August 2008.

20. PricewaterhouseCoopers, World Economic Forum on East Asia, briefing material, Singapore, 24–25 June 2007, p. 11.

Kazutoshi Chatani is a technical officer at the International Labour Office (ILO) Jakarta office.

Kee Beom Kim is Labour Economist at the Regional Office for Asia and the Pacific of the International Labour Office (ILO) in Bangkok.

4
WHAT CAN ASEAN DO TO ADDRESS RISING POVERTY LEVELS AND SOCIAL UNREST?

Lim Teck Ghee

Introduction

The topic "What can ASEAN do to address rising poverty levels and social unrest" is especially pertinent if the current global economic crisis is prolonged or worsens further. Even if the crisis abates during the next year, various forecasts point to a slower rate of growth in the ASEAN national economies. Continuing ripple effects on various economic sectors, socioeconomic groups and local areas already badly hit as a result of the worsening economic conditions during the past eighteen months can be expected for some time to come. To ensure that economic distress does not translate into sharply rising poverty levels and social unrest, policy-makers in the region will need to be more proactive than they have been to date — both at the regional and national levels.

Unfortunately, at the regional level, the outcome of the most recent meeting of the Heads of State/Government of the ASEAN member states in Cha-am Hua Hin on 1 March 2009 to discuss the global economic and financial crisis — has provided little evidence or assurance that the governments at the regional level are focused on addressing the poverty and social impacts of the crisis. The press communiqué arising out of the meeting mainly affirmed "the necessity of proactive and decisive policy actions to restore market confidence and [to] ensure continued financial stability to promote sustainable regional economic growth". Emphasis was placed on "expansionary macroeconomic policies, including fiscal stimulus, monetary easing, access to credit including trade financing, and measures to support private sector, particularly small and medium enterprises (SMEs) undertaken by each ASEAN Member State to stimulate domestic demand". Although the importance of "coordinating policies and taking joint actions that would be mutually reinforcing at the regional level" was mentioned, this was more focused on the regional grouping's "determination to ensure the free flow of goods, services and investment, and facilitate movement of business persons, professionals, talents and labour, and freer flow of capital" rather than on alleviating the regional poverty and social impacts arising from the crisis.

In all, the meeting appears to have taken a hands-off approach in terms of a regional approach to the challenge of worsening poverty in the region arising from the global crisis, preferring — or at least it seems to the public — to opt for the national governments to deal with the impact in their own ways. Both at the national and regional levels, it is also noticeable that the immediate response packages to the crisis have been more directed towards stimulating growth and shoring up the banking, finance and manufacturing sectors with considerably less attention given to strengthening the social safety net and the introduction of special social protection programmes.[1] In the last few months, government in the region have stitched together a hodge-podge of modest social protection programmes in their fiscal stimulus response to the crisis but there is still little evidence of substantive efforts at formulating and implementing policies that can systematically address the problem of rising poverty (see Table 4.1).

Some Major Concerns When Addressing Poverty Impact

What are the main concerns that should be uppermost on the minds of national and regional policy-makers as they grapple with the economic crisis? There are at least three key sets of concerns which the region and affected countries may want to prioritize in policy-making and planning. The first relates to the impact on poverty numbers and poverty levels? How many in the countries and region are affected? Who are affected and where are they to be found? The second relates to the major ways in which the poor are affected by the crisis, and the types of remedial measures that can be of greatest benefit to the poor. This set also includes concerns on how to ensure that stabilization or social safety net assistance to regions, sectors and communities are well designed and robust and are not affected by political bias or other forms of distortion that will reduce their efficiency and impact. Especially important to address is how to ensure that social safety net measures do not suffer from leakage, bias or are undermined by high administrative costs. The last set of concerns relates to the relationship between poverty, inequality and the larger political economy in the longer run. This set is more complex than the first two and can cover a wide range of questions including:

- How much priority should governments give to issues of redistribution during a period of prolonged economic recession or crisis and/or when government revenues are sharply reduced.
- How to ensure that spatial, occupational and group

TABLE 4.1

Selected Fiscal Stimulus Packages in Southeast Asian Region

	Size	Salient Features
Indonesia	Rp 71.3 trillion (US$6.1 billion); 1.4% of 2008 GDP (budget deficit in 2008: 1.2% of GDP)	Tax breaks for individuals and companies (Rp 43 trillion); waived import (budget duties and taxes (Rp 13.3 trillion); infrastructure spending (Rp 10.2 trillion); diesel subsidy (Rp 2.8 trillion); rural development (Rp 0.6 trillion).
		Announced in January 2009; enhances a previous Rp 27.5 trillion stimulus package.
Malaysia	RM 7 billion (US$1.9 billion); 1% of 2008 GDP (budget deficit in 2008: 5.1% of GDP)	Investment funds to promote strategic industries and high-speed broadband (RM 1.9 billion); small-scale projects such as village roads, school repairs (RM 1.6 billion); affordable housing (RM 1.5 billion); education and skills training programmes (RM 1 billion); public transport and military facilities (RM 1 billion).
		Announced in November 2008; a second stimulus package was expected in February 2009.
Philippines	P 330 billion (US$6.5 billion); 4.6% of 2008 GDP (budget deficit in 2008: 0.8% of GDP)	Increased in expenditures (P 160 billion); infra-structure (P 100 billion); tax relief and reduction of corporate income tax rate (P 40 billion); waiver of penalties on loans from social security institutions (P 30 billion).

		Announced in January 2009; specific details not available at the time of writing.
Singapore	S$20.5 billion (US$13.7 billion); 11.5% of 2008 GDP (budget surplus in 2008: 0.9% of GDP)	Job credit programme: cash transfers for employers to cover part of their wage bills and avoid mass lay-offs (S$4.5 billion); special risk sharing initiative: Government guarantees working-capital loans (up to S$5 million) to individual firms to stimulate bank lending; cut in corporate tax rate from 18% to 17%; and personal income tax rebates of 20% of taxes due (capped at S$2,000).
		Announced in January 2009; the Government plans to draw S$4.9 billion from previously accumulated reserves to finance the job credit and special risk sharing initiative programmes, and will also tap reserves held by the Monetary Authority of Singapore (the central bank) and the Government of Singapore Investment Corporation (a sovereign wealth fund).
Thailand	B 115 billion (US$3.3 billion); 1.2% of 2008 GDP (fiscal deficit in 2008: 1.4% of GDP)	One-time distribution of B 2,000 in cash to people who currently earn monthly salaries of less than B 15,000; support for social security; free education programmes; job creation; and low-interest loans to farmers.

continued on next page

TABLE 4.1 — *cont'd*

	Size	*Salient Features*
Thailand		Approved by the cabinet in January 2009, the initiative extends by six months a package of economic stimulus measures implemented by the previous government, including such measures as, lower water and electricity charges, free rides on some of Bangkok's public buses and free third-class train rides nationwide.
Vietnam	D 17 trillion (US$1 billion); 1.2% of 2008 GDP (fiscal deficit in 2008: 4.1% of GDP)	Details not announced at the time of writing. Components include: subsidized loans to farmers at an annual rate of 11.5%; a 4% subsidy on the interest rate enterprises pay for their loans; and credit for small businesses.
		Announced in December 2008.

Source: ESCAP, *Economic and Social Survey of Asia and the Pacific 2009*, United Nations, New York, 2009, p. 142.

disparities are more efficiently addressed so that rising poverty does not lead to the destabilization of the economy or society.

The Numbers Issue: How Many More Poor?

On the first set which relates to estimates or measurement or the impact of the crisis on income levels, livelihoods and welfare, no data is available yet of the increase in poverty numbers for the ASEAN region partly because the crisis is still in the process of unfolding. However, the major international development agencies working in the Asian and ASEAN region are in general agreement that the impact of the crisis has plunged a very large number of people into poverty. According to a February report from the International Labour Organization (ILO), as many as 23 million people could lose their jobs in Asia whilst more than 140 million could fall into poverty. These figures cover the entire Asian region but they have not been accompanied by disaggregated country breakdowns. During the same month, the World Bank also issued a policy note entitled "The Global Economic Crisis: Assessing Vulnerability with a Poverty Lens" on the impact of the crisis. According to the bank's new estimates for 2009, lower economic growth rates will trap 46 million more people on less than US$1.25 a day than was expected prior to the crisis. An extra 53 million are expected to stay trapped on less than US$2 a day. This, according to the bank, is on top of the 130–155 million people pushed into poverty in 2008 because of soaring food and fuel prices. In country terms, it was estimated that almost 40 per cent of 107 developing countries were highly exposed to the poverty effects of the crisis and the remainder was moderately exposed, with less than 10 per cent facing little risk.

Identifying Priority Poverty Groups

Because the incidence of poverty and related socioeconomic deprivation within the ASEAN region and at least eight of the region's ten countries are so large, it will be necessary for policy-makers to prioritize which groups within the total population of the poor should require urgent attention. On this issue, it may be useful at least in planning terms to distinguish between the two major groups of poor that will need attention — the traditional poor and the new poor. The traditional poor are those that have long comprised the bottom strata of the income and occupational distribution in the ASEAN countries. These are primarily people who live in rural areas and are unemployed or underemployed or work in the lowest rung of the agricultural or urban sectors. The new poor consist of those who may have managed to climb above the poverty line but have now tumbled back below it as a result of the loss of jobs or income arising from the crisis. In the region as a whole, those most affected by recent job and income losses include the following:[2]

- "Flexible"/migrant/undocumented foreign workforce;
- Contract workers or overtime dependent workers;
- Retrenched workers at the lower occupational rungs;
- Agricultural sector workers and owners of small agricultural holdings;
- Manufacturing sector workers;
- Unemployed graduates, new entrants and underskilled workers; and
- Self-employed, especially those severely affected by the ripple effects arising from the economic slowdown or recessionary conditions.

Obviously not all who are identified as belonging to these groups fall into the category of the poor. Higher skilled manufacturing sector workers, unemployed graduates and more highly remunerated self-employed generally fall into the middle or higher income categories. They will have a greater capacity to withstand the challenges of the economic downturn on their own and could well do without the need for special state assistance.

National approaches in identifying poverty groups impacted by the economic crisis will vary considerably but all will need to take into account the key criterion of exclusion from productive resources, decent work and social security; as well as extreme vulnerability to higher food and fuel costs.[3] Careful targeting can separate out the most vulnerable in key socioeconomic and occupational groupings that have been affected from those who are better able to fend for themselves in coping with the loss of employment or income. Such targeting is necessary to ensure that the stimulus packages or remedial measures do in fact reach the most deserving and most needy amongst the traditional and the new poor, and are not deployed on groups or sectors that have the capacity and ability to overcome the dislocation without the need for outside assistance.

Social Safety Net, Employment or Other Forms of Assistance

The next set of questions relates to what needs to be done to alleviate the plight of the poverty groups affected by the crisis. Here again, various approaches are available to policy-makers. In the recent policy recommendations advanced by the various international development agencies to address the poverty impact of the crisis, what is discernible is the (understandable) tendency for each agency to prioritize approaches that are related to the mandate and work programmes of the agency concerned. Thus the ILO has emphasized that the crisis is likely to lead to stagnant or falling real wages, with the potential for increased incidence of wage related disputes. It has also warned that the crisis was quickly evolving "into an employment and social crisis" with the region at the tipping point of seeing social unrest explode into the streets, as the jobless and marginalized demand greater government action.[4] To avert this social unrest, the ILO has recommended that "social partners should be included in policy discussions in order to make sure that the most vulnerable and affected people are given the central attention". Amongst some of the ILOs priority policy prescriptions are programmes to protect employment and support household purchasing power, public expenditure on schools, hospitals and healthcare, and the boosting of worker skills for longer-term productivity.[5]

For the World Bank, the crisis has highlighted the serious threat to the achievement of the UN's Millennium Development Goals (MDGs), to which it is committed with specific targets to overcome poverty by 2015. According to the bank's research, the sharply lower economic growth rates will significantly retard progress in reducing infant mortality, for example. According to preliminary estimates for 2009 to 2015, an average 200,000 to 400,000 more children a year, a total of 1.4 to 2.8 million, may die if the crisis persists. The bank's recent policy note on the impact of the global crisis also emphasized that it was critical for exposed countries to finance job creation, the delivery of essential services and infrastructure, and safety net programmes for the vulnerable. At the same time, the bank has cautioned that up to three quarters of these countries cannot raise funds domestically or internationally to finance programmes to curb the effects of the downturn.

One quarter of the exposed countries also lacked the institutional capacity to expand spending to protect vulnerable groups. To meet this shortfall, the bank note has urged financial support in the form of grants and low or zero interest loans for these countries. It has also called for the establishment of a "Vulnerability Fund" in which each developed country devotes 0.7 per cent of its stimulus package to the fund. Three priority areas for the bank proposed Vulnerability Fund are: safety net programmes, infrastructure investments, and support for small and medium-sized enterprises and microfinance institutions.

A different tack on the approach necessary to alleviate the impact of the crisis can be arrived at if the results of a recent study undertaken by the Institute of Development Studies (IDS) are given serious consideration. Drawing on empirical work undertaken in Bangladesh, Indonesia, Kenya, Jamaica and Zambia, the study established that people living in the world's poorest communities are eating less frequently and consuming worse food as a result of the global financial crisis (*The Guardian*, 27 March 2009). "Eating less frequently and less diverse and nutrient-rich foods was commonly reported", the report states. Many poor people reported not being able to makes ends meet. Managing food, health and educational needs has been a struggle, and not only for the very poorest. Secondly, many poor families hit by the economic downturn are also removing their children from school and pushing them into work much earlier. For some, particularly young children, the impacts may be permanent: children who drop out of school to work or because their parents cannot afford fees, books or breakfast, are unlikely to re-enrol even if food prices begin to decline. Researchers stressed that it was difficult to untangle which aspects of hardship could be directly traced to either the current economic crisis, the fuel and food price rise of the previous year or the local political situation.

At the same time — drawing from studies of the impact of previous recessions — the IDS concluded that "poverty, malnutrition and infant mortality increased during every national financial crisis in the past 11 years".

Whatever the programmatic approach and strategy — whether it is a focus on food security or on employment generation; whether the target groups are women or the most vulnerable amongst the young and elderly — governments need to act quickly since prolonged deprivation and the associated impact on health and physical and economic well being could result in the inter-generational reproduction of poverty, making it more intractable to resolve if it is permitted to languish or grow. In fact this is probably the most serious outcome of deepening poverty — the silent and insidious erosion or reversal of past gains in key health and other well-being indicators.

Lessons from the 1997 Crisis and from Best Practices in Poverty Alleviation

The last set of concerns relates to the effects of rising and entrenched poverty in a context of prolonged economic recession or crisis. Here, lessons from the region's experience with the last economic crisis in 1997 are instructive.[6] Firstly, it should be noted that the negative effects on poverty generally extend beyond the period of the crisis itself. Although economic growth resumed fairly quickly after the 1997 crisis, in some countries it took as long as ten years to recover lost ground in the national efforts to reduce poverty.[7] Secondly, the increase in poverty is likely to bring about increased inequality. Income inequality levels in the ASEAN countries as measured by the gini coefficient of inequality are already amongst some of the highest amongst countries in the world, and an increase in inequality is not only unacceptable socially and politically, but it could also very well generate severe socioeconomic dislocation and pain with attendant costs to the larger economy and society. Thirdly, the potential for social unrest is especially pronounced in urban areas — not only in the megacities but also in the smaller and equally crowded secondary cities. In these urban settings, the volatile combination of urban slums and squatters where the poor are concentrated, a growing unemployed population of low-income wage workers and self-employed (including foreign and local migrant workers), and widening disparities and inequalities of income and wealth could very well prove to be the spark to ignite a tinderbox of dissatisfaction and unrest.

Other lessons in tackling entrenched poverty systematically and efficiently have long been available. Some of these lessons[8] include the following:

- They emphasize women's agency role in the development activity through a range of new freedoms such as the freedom for women to work outside home, the freedom to earn an independent income, the freedom to have ownership rights, and the freedom to receive education. Beyond this, the focus on women has had an important (though underestimated but not yet well-studied) impact on reducing the inter-generational reproduction of poverty.
- There is relatively open access to information and transparency in decision-making. Once information and knowledge are accessed by poor communities, it places them on a more equal footing when negotiating with others as well as enables them to realize their full developmental potential.
- They are often based on government-NGO-CBO (community-based organizations) partnerships or coalitions for change with project activities more geared towards control of

resources and decisions by local communities than by outside parties.

- They have moved from project, periodic, supply-led and output driven approaches to programmatic, continuous involvement, demand-driven and outcomes-oriented approaches. In some of the cases below, considerable upscaling and replication have taken place of initially modest or small projects.

- They have ensured that sustainability is a key outcome through investments in networks of the poor and through the creation of organizational capabilities that have worked for the benefit of the many rather than the few.

- Although initially focused on the creation of social capital, they have been able to bring about the rapid transformation of social capital into economic capital. This is particularly noticeable when comparing the East Asian with the South Asian experience where, in the case of the latter region, many initiatives have remained limited in their impacts as a result of the failure to move to the next stage of development after the achievement of social development gains.

- Exit strategies have been mainstreamed into project design through effective cost recovery approaches, review of grant/ subsidy components, and monitoring systems to ensure optimization of grant/subsidy impact.

- Graft, leakage and corruption are major obstacles to progress.

- Bureaucratic elites in collaboration with political elites — rather than the traditional bogeymen of middlemen and private sector intermediaries — are just as or even more likely to cream off poorly designed and monitored programmes.

Conclusion

The most important lesson perhaps to bear in mind is that the scourge of poverty can be successfully combated even in the most depressed of conditions. Often though, it is precisely the great wealth of technical expertise and human resources brought to bear on anti-poverty work — especially in terms of the administrative apparatus used for planning, processing and targeting — that turns out to be a liability by diverting resources from the important work of empowering the poor and unblocking access for the needy. This problem is compounded by leakages through inefficient or corrupt practices. At the end of the day, it is the intangibles that result in desirable outcomes in anti-poverty work, namely the combination of strong political will, good governance, empowerment of the poor, commitment and stamina, and focused and targeted idealism, rather than technical inputs.

Notes

1. In Malaysia, the government's first stimulus measure to cushion the shock was to increase the capitalization of a government investment company by US$5 billion, in part to stabilize the stock exchange. The move was heavily criticized by the major workers union in the country which argued that the government agency disbursing the funds "is the custodian of people's money" and "not the ATM for the government" to bail out state-linked firms. "This is the hard-earned money of the workers, their retirement plan. How is this bailout plan going to benefit the workers?" See Lim Teck Ghee, "Global Economic Crisis and Impact on Malaysia", presentation to Malaysian Parliamentarians, Kuala Lumpur, 29 October 2008.

2. The listing here is based on a Malaysian country presentation on the "Global Economic Crisis and Impact on Malaysia". See Lim

Teck Ghee, "Global Economic Crisis and Impact on Malaysia", presentation to Malaysian Parliamentarians, Kuala Lumpur, 29 October 2008.

3. According to the latest UNESCAP annual report, "when people are affected by sudden shocks, the ones most at risk are the poor, women who are labourers in the manufacturing sector, the youngest and oldest populations and socially excluded groups." Not only have these groups fewer resources such as real assets and savings to cushion the shocks, "but they also have less influence on economic and political decision making". See "Economic and Social Survey of Asia and the Pacific 2009 — Addressing Triple Threats to Development", United Nations, New York, 2009, p. 13.

4. Migrant workers with short-term contracts as well as women working in small- and medium-sized factories and firms are particularly vulnerable. "From India to China to Vietnam, large numbers of internal migrants have lost their jobs, generating a reverse migration to the countryside in search of rural employment", Yamamoto said.

5. The ILO's policy recommendations appear to be in line with or supported by the major regional developmental agency, the Asian Development Bank. According to the ADB's Vice President for Sustainable Development, Ursula Schaefer-Preus, any stimulus packages would need to include job creation and infrastructure needs that will most benefit the poor. See <http://www.google.com/hostednews/afp/article/ALeqM5jYxfcKF30-iYHsHUv5GVXUS10F3Q>.

6. A recent ADB media note issued in connection with a forthcoming high-level policy meeting to evaluate the impact of the global economic slowdown on poverty and sustainable development in Asia and the Pacific has stated that "the causes and impacts are different from the Asian Financial Crisis in 1998 in several respects. The current crisis concerns not only the very poor (i.e. those living under the US$1.25 poverty line) but more so the vulnerable poor, mostly educated youth in the export sectors (and backward

industries and services). Impact channels are going through labour markets, migration and remittances, social budgets, social protection, gender, health, education and training, among others." See <http://www.adb.org/Documents/Events/2009/Poverty-Social-Development/default.asp>.

7. ILO, *Global Wage Report 2008/2009.*

8. This is drawn from Lim Teck Ghee, "Best Practices in Poverty Reduction in the UNESCAP Region", unpublished note, 2005.

References

ESCAP. *Economic and Social Survey of Asia and the Pacific 2009.* United Nations, New York, 2009.

<http://web.worldbank.org/WBSITE/EXTERNAL/NEWS/0,,contentMDK: 22067892~pagePK:64257043~piPK:437376~theSitePK:4607,00.html>.

<http://www.adb.org/Documents/Events/2009/Poverty-Social-Development/default.asp http://www.google.com/hostednews/afp/article/ALeqM5jYxfcKF30-iYHsHUv5GVXUS10F3Q>.

ILO. *Labour and Social Trends in Asia and the Pacific 2007.* Bangkok, 2007.

————. *Global Wage Report 2008/2009.* Geneva, 2008.

Lim, Teck Ghee. "Best Practices in Poverty Reduction in the UNESCAP Region". Unpublished note, 2005.

————. "Global Economic Crisis and Impact on Malaysia". Presentation to Malaysian Parliamentarians, Kuala Lumpur, 29 October 2008.

UNDP. *Human Development Report 2007/2008.* New York, 2007.

Lim Teck Ghee is a Professorial Fellow at the Malaysian Institute of Asian and Development Studies, UCSI University.

5
ASEAN: THE REGION'S FINANCIAL SECTOR AMID THE PERFECT STORM[1]

Hui Cheung Tai

A Rough Ride, but the Ship is still Intact

A decade after the Asian financial crisis, the reforms and progress achieved in ASEAN's economies[2] and financial sectors have been severely tested by the global economic and financial turmoil originating from the developed world. The collapse in investor risk appetite and economic activity globally threatened to wreak financial havoc on ASEAN once again. More than six months after the collapse of Lehman Brothers, the key turning point in the current global crisis, ASEAN financial and banking systems remain structurally solid, according to available data. Yet while the region's financial institutions have survived the first wave of the global financial storm, considerable challenges lie ahead in the months, quarters, and possibly years ahead. The aftermath of the storm is likely to put the region's financial system to new tests, both from cyclical and a structural perspective.

This report shares our observations of how ASEAN's financial and banking sectors have coped with the global financial and economic turmoil, and provide our thoughts on what can be expected in the medium term. The first part examines the impact of the global financial and economic crisis on ASEAN's financial and banking sectors between September 2008 and May 2009 via a number of channels, including foreign-exchange movements and trends, equities, fixed income, and credit. We look at the effects of risk aversion and the U.S. dollar liquidity squeeze on the region's banking sectors and lending behaviour.

The second part discusses the outlook for ASEAN's financial and banking sectors as the crisis continues to unfold. There are some early signs of economic stabilization in developed economies, and Asian exports appear to have bottomed. Global investor risk appetite also seems to have begun a steady recovery. The return of international capital should provide some relief to the region — but too much of a good thing can also create challenges in the future, such as overvaluation of financial assets. Meanwhile, the negative effects of the economic down-cycle on ASEAN's banking industry and financial markets, such as a rise in non-performing assets, may persist for some time. And the global regulatory landscape is also likely to change, which will impact the region's banking sectors both directly and indirectly.

In summary, while ASEAN's financial markets and banks have suffered considerable negative impact from the global financial crisis, the damage has been manageable. This implies that the reforms undertaken by the region's governments, central banks, and regulators since the Asian financial crisis have put these economies and their financial industries on sounder footing. That said, this momentum will need to continue, as a fresh round of global financial regulatory reform is already underway.

How Rough was the Ride?

The global financial turmoil led to considerable volatility in ASEAN's financial and banking sectors. The extent of this volatility is examined by drawing data from a number of markets, including foreign exchange, equities, interest rates, fixed income, and credit. Although the global financial and economic turbulence is likely to persist for some time and will continue to affect the region in bouts, we use data available through the end of May 2009, since it captures the initial shocks following the collapse of Lehman Brothers — which is generally seen as the "game-changing" event that led to the U.S. dollar liquidity crunch and global investor risk aversion.

The region's markets have been affected by common themes, which are in turn linked to troubles in the developed economies. Several factors reduced foreign investors' appetite for ASEAN financial assets:

1.   Given the uncertainty about the financial system stability and the economic outlook, investors in the developed world switched into "safe-haven" financial assets. This led to capital outflows from emerging markets, including ASEAN.

2.   For leveraged investors, the need for cash to meet margin calls as asset values declined exacerbated these capital outflows.

3.   Concerns about ASEAN's economic outlook as a result of falling demand for the region's exports from the developed world prompted investors to exit their positions. There were also worries that the global financial crisis could undermine ASEAN's structural stability via the financial and banking sectors.

Equities — Hefty Losses, Swift Rebound

Even before the collapse of Lehman Brothers, ASEAN equity markets were already consolidating throughout much of 2008. The MSCI Asia ex-Japan index reached its peak in early November 2007, and the region's individual indices also peaked around that time. As Table 5.1 shows, from these peaks until the Lehman Brothers collapse on 15 September 2008, individual stock indices

TABLE 5.1

Regional Equity Benchmark Performance

(in local-currency terms)

	Singapore	Thailand	Malaysia	Indonesia	Philippines	Vietnam	MSCI Asia ex-Japan
Cyclical peak to Lehman collapse	−32.9%	−28.5%	−31.1%	−36.3%	−31.7%	−59.3%	−41.3%
Lehman collapse to cyclical trough	−43.3%	−41.3%	−20.6%	−38.4%	−35.6%	−50.5%	−42.7%
Peak to trough	−62.0%	−58.0%	−45.3%	−60.7%	−56.0%	−79.9%	−66.4%
Asian financial crisis	−62.0%	−85.3%	−79.3%	−65.3%	−68.6%	N/A	−66.6%

Source: Bloomberg, SCB Global Research.

had already lost between 28.5 per cent (Thailand) and 59.3 per cent (Vietnam). Following the Lehman collapse, the decline continued until the end of Q1-2009. Between 15 September 2008 and the trough in Q1-2009, regional stock markets declined between 20.6 per cent (Malaysia) and 50.5 per cent (Vietnam).

From peak to trough (January 2007 to April 2009), regional equity indices fell between 45.3 per cent (Malaysia) and 79.9 per cent (Vietnam). In Vietnam's case, one can argue that the particularly sharp drop was exacerbated by a stock market bubble and the authorities' efforts to deflate it. In other markets, the magnitude of equity market declines during this period was comparable to those during the Asian financial crisis for Singapore and Indonesia, but much milder for Thailand, Malaysia, and the Philippines. Since mid-March, renewed market confidence has been driving regional equity performance. By late May, Malaysia and Indonesia had seen their benchmark indices return to pre-Lehman levels.

FIGURE 5.1
Regional Benchmark Equity Index Performance
(15 September 2008 = 100)

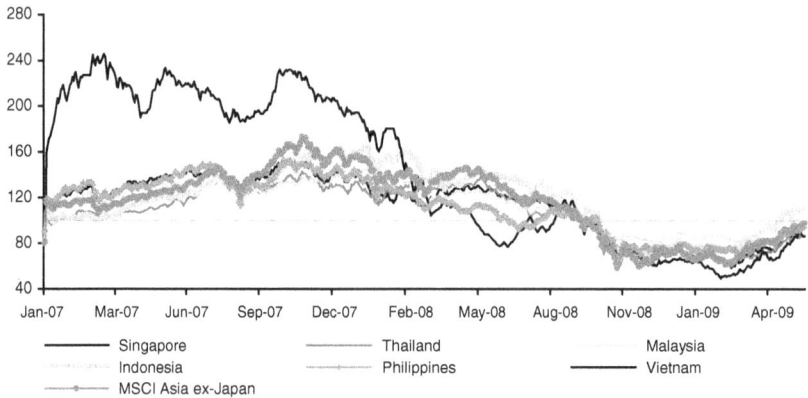

Source: Bloomberg, SCB Global Research.

Foreign Exchange — Strong Fundamentals Limit Volatility

ASEAN currencies have been less volatile than regional equity markets during the current crisis. In the first half of 2008, most ASEAN currencies were under pressure to appreciate due to trade surpluses and expectations that central banks would tolerate stronger exchange rates and tighten monetary policy to combat rising inflation. The prevailing market expectation at the time was for this ASEAN currency strength to persist into H2-2008. However, as inflationary pressures started to subside with the peaking of food and energy prices in August 2008, and as ASEAN exports showed early signs of weakness, the region's currencies began to lose support against the U.S. dollar (USD). Between July 2008 and April 2009 (see Figure 5.2), the THB and VND lost just over 8 per

FIGURE 5.2

Regional Currencies' Performance *versus* USD

(July 2008 to April 2009)

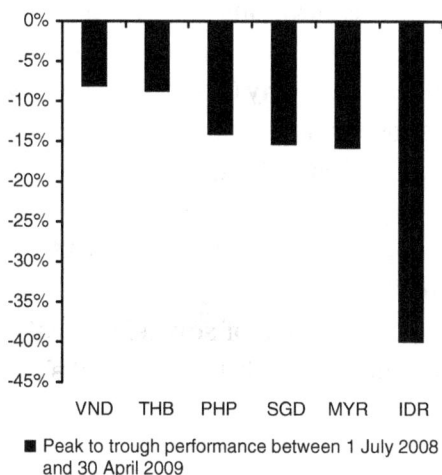

Peak to trough performance between 1 July 2008 and 30 April 2009

Source: Bloomberg, SCB Global Research.

cent against the USD. The MYR, SGD, and PHP lost between 14 per cent and 16 per cent. The IDR was hit the hardest — investor concerns regarding the country's ability to meet its external liabilities caused the currency to drop almost 40 per cent against the greenback. In October and November 2008, the IDR weakened from 9,500 to 12,100 against the USD.

Even taking into account the sizeable IDR drop, ASEAN currencies' reaction to the current economic turmoil has been limited compared with the declines seen during the Asian financial crisis. Sizeable foreign reserve positions built up after the Asian financial crisis give central banks a means to stabilize their currencies and bolster investor confidence in their external debt

positions. The healthy current account positions of most ASEAN
economies (see Figure 5.3) have also helped. Support from other
governments (in the form of bilateral swap line agreements) and
from international organizations such as the Asian Development
Bank and the World Bank has further reinforced confidence. At
the end of Q1-2009 and in early Q2-2009, ASEAN currencies found
a footing and subsequently stabilized as global investor risk
appetite appeared to find a floor.

Fixed Income Market — Policy Rates Set the Trend

In analysing the performance of sovereign local-currency bonds,
the six ASEAN countries with better-established bond markets

FIGURE 5.3

Current Account Balance as Percentage of GDP

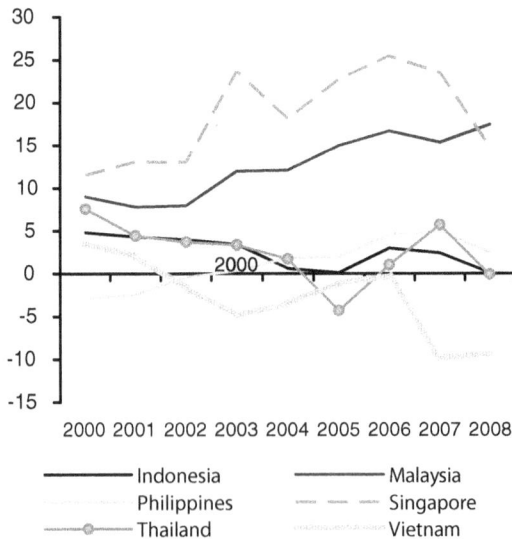

Source: IMF, SCB Global Research.

can be divided into two broad groups. The first group — Singapore, Malaysia, Vietnam, and Thailand — saw government bond yield curves shift lower in September and October, as inflation had peaked and their central banks were expected to ease monetary policy to support growth. The second group — Indonesia and the Philippines — initially saw their government bond yields rise in late September and October 2008 on investor risk aversion, in particular concerns about the countries' ability to meet their external liabilities amid weakening exchange rates. Yet this fear faded, and government bond yields in these two markets fell in line with the regional trend.

As the region's governments step up fiscal stimulus to support their economies, there have been concerns that government bond supply may surge, leading to possible downgrades in sovereign credit ratings. This caused some pick-up in government bond

FIGURE 5.4
USD Bond Issuance in Asia

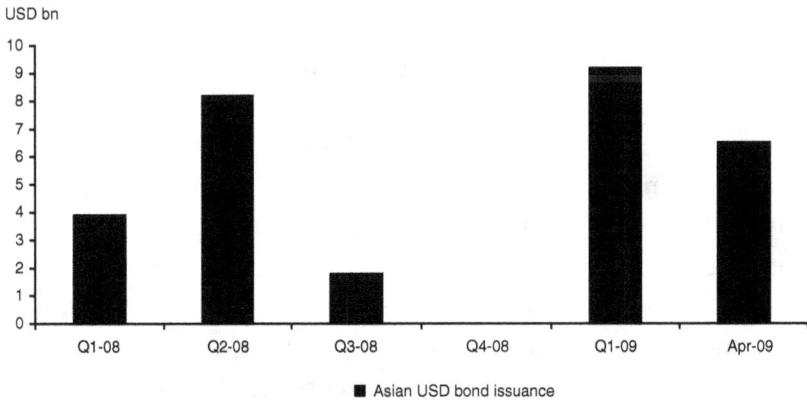

Source: SCB Global Research.

yields, especially at the long end of the curve. In terms of issuance, risk aversion and the liquidity crunch negatively impacted the sovereign and corporate markets in Q4-2008, in both U.S. dollar and local currency. The good news is that successful U.S. dollar sovereign issues from the Philippines and Indonesia in Q1-2009 indicate a return of investor appetite. They also reflect a good understanding of market demand on the part of the issuers, as the tenors and issuance size were managed accordingly to ensure a warm reception.

Sovereign Credit Default Swaps (CDS) — Dictated by Risk Appetite

The collapse of Lehman Brothers triggered a wave of risk aversion, as reflected in the sharp surge in sovereign credit default swap (CDS) spreads, a gauge of market expectations of sovereign default risk. Following a spike in mid-September 2008, ASEAN CDS spreads have been highly volatile but have remained on a downtrend (see Figure 5.5). By the end of May 2009, most, if not all, sovereign CDS spreads had returned to pre-Lehman levels, though they are still elevated relative to their levels between 2007 and H1-2008.

We believe the surge in CDS spreads is more a reflection of weak investor risk appetite than of a genuine deterioration in ASEAN sovereign credit quality. While the depreciation in some Asian currencies did put additional stress on those countries' ability to repay their foreign currency debt, most ASEAN countries have sufficient foreign exchange reserves or bilateral swap lines they can draw upon for foreign currency if necessary. Nonetheless, the widening of sovereign CDS spreads does reflect the previous difficulties ASEAN members faced in raising foreign currency debt, and the narrowing of spreads indicates an easing of such tensions.

FIGURE 5.5

Movements in Sovereign CDS Spreads (USD 5Y Senior)

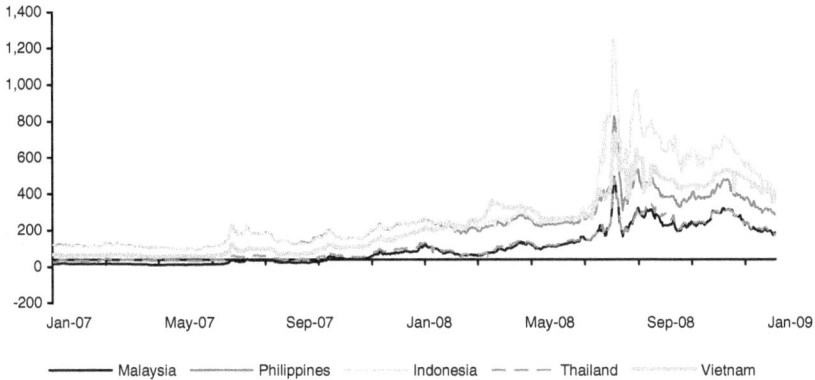

Source: Bloomberg, SCB Global Research.

Interbank Liquidity — Tight in USD, Ample in Local Currencies

A chronic shortage of U.S. dollar liquidity has been a prominent feature of the current financial crisis. A lack of trust amongst financial institutions globally has led to considerable hoarding of U.S. dollar liquidity, despite relief measures implemented by central banks in developed economies (that is, enlarging their balance sheets). Quantifying the shortage of U.S. dollar liquidity within ASEAN is challenging, as public information is not readily available.

We use the spread between central bank policy rates and local-currency interbank market rates as a proxy for the local liquidity environment (see Figure 5.6).[3] The stable spreads for Thailand and Malaysia reflect that their central banks managed to maintain a stable local-currency liquidity environment. We believe the same is true for Singapore, despite the fact that it executes its

FIGURE 5.6
Spread between Central Bank Policy Rates and
1M Interbank Market Rates

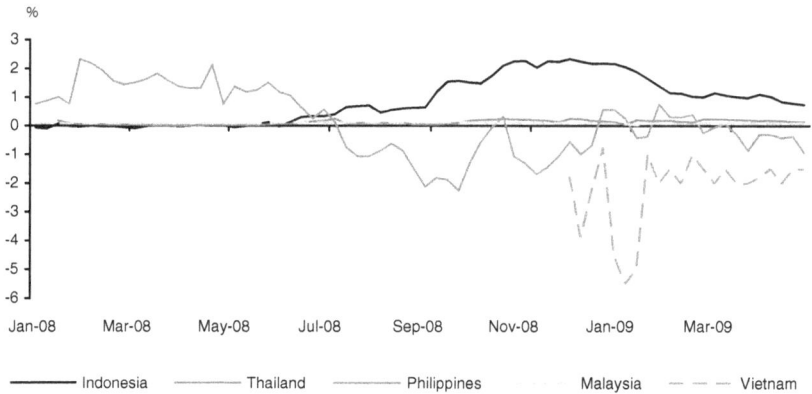

Source: Bloomberg, SCB Global Research.

monetary policy via the exchange rate rather than using a policy rate. In the Philippines and Vietnam, the central banks are also able to provide ample local currency to ensure liquidity. This is reflected in the fact that these countries' interbank market rates have been below their official policy rates for much of the post-Lehman period. Indonesia is the only country which saw the spread between its interbank market rate and its policy rate widen in Q4-2009, but this has eased since the turn of the year.

Bank Lending — Cutback in Demand and Supply

A clear deceleration in bank lending growth was seen in four ASEAN economies — Singapore, Indonesia, Thailand, and the Philippines (see Figure 5.7) — until March/April 2009. These

FIGURE 5.7
Total Lending Growth, Year-on-Year

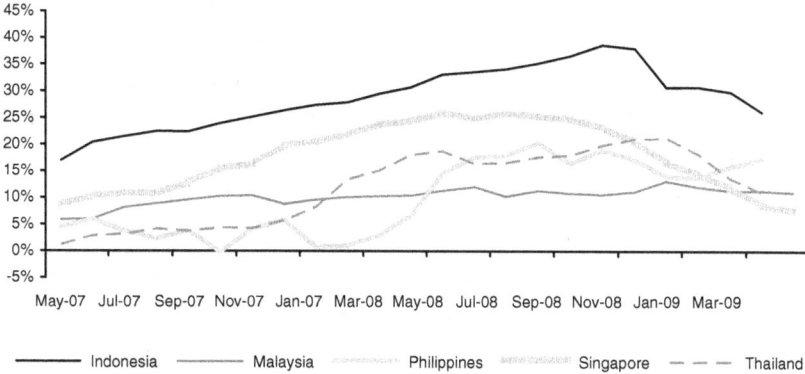

Source: CEIC, SCB Global Research.

countries' total outstanding bank loans have actually contracted since the beginning of 2009. Malaysia is an exception — its year-on-year lending growth has been consistent into 2009, and its total loans outstanding have continued to expand. This can be explained by the lower degree of volatility in Malaysian lending over the past two years. Across most ASEAN countries, trade finance is another area where the business sector has found it difficult to obtain funding. In addition to a decline in the absolute quantity of lending, banks have also shifted to a preference for letters of credit over open accounts due to concerns about counterparty risk.

A slowdown in lending is natural in a cyclical slowdown and can be explained by both demand- and supply-side factors:

1. Financial institutions have faced a considerable liquidity crunch (especially in USD), during this crisis, and the need

to preserve liquidity and protect capital has forced them to scale back lending and manage their balance sheets very conservatively. This applies to lending to corporates, individuals, and other financial institutions.

2. Given the prevailing economic conditions and the possible deterioration in credit quality, financial institutions have taken a more cautious lending stance enforced tighter risk management.

3. Foreseeing a decline in orders and a drop in revenue, corporate borrowers have postponed or cancelled investment plans to preserve cash flow.

4. Where possible, debts are being repaid to reduce interest charges. Leverage for financial investment has also been reduced as financial assets in the region fall in value.

5. The decline in commodity prices also implies that the value of trade financing required is reduced.

Points 1 and 2 represent supply-side constraints to lending, while points 3–5 are more demand-side factors leading to weaker lending growth, or outright contraction. To tackle the supply-side issues, authorities in the region have introduced initiatives aimed at sharing such credit risk, and hence encouraging banks to extend lending. These initiatives often target lending to SMEs, since this group of borrowers is often the most vulnerable in an economic downturn, with lenders reducing their credit lines substantially.

Foreign bank lending has also fallen substantially in the ASEAN region as U.S., U.K., and European banks rein in lending to preserve capital. In H2-2008, according to BIS statistics, foreign banks reduced lending by a total of US$86.3 billion in ASEAN-6, accounting for 11.9 per cent of total lending by foreign banks in the region. Singapore and Malaysia suffered the biggest declines in lending by foreign banks during the period, at US$49.2 billion and US$22.2 billion, respectively. This trend could continue as international banks, under pressure to shrink their balance sheets further, continue to consolidate their international activities.

The Damage thus Far is Manageable

Based on the financial market and banking sector data outlined above, we believe that the global financial and economic turmoil has had a significant, but manageable, impact on ASEAN's financial and banking sectors. Direct losses due to exposure to "sub-prime" or other toxic financial assets appear limited. The damage to equity markets in the wake of the Lehman Brothers collapse was considerable, and in some cases comparable to the Asian financial crisis. The good news is that the return of investor risk appetite is facilitating an equally strong rebound in Q2-2009. With the exception of the IDR, the impact on exchange rates was small. Any negative reaction in local government bond markets was brief at the peak of the crisis, as aggressive rate cuts by the region's central banks helped to push government bond yields lower and overcome investor risk aversion. Commercial banks' more conservative lending approach has also prompted them to put more of their assets into government paper, supporting bond prices.

The slowdown in economic activity is likely to have a more prolonged impact than the financial turbulence on commercial banks. The U.S. dollar liquidity crunch, higher default risk, and weaker borrowing appetite have all weakened lending growth, and in some cases caused an outright contraction in lending. This will have a direct impact on both global trade and capital expenditure plans.

Hence, the negative impact of the first wave of global financial market turmoil on ASEAN was manageable, although some sectors, such as SMEs, have faced more difficulties obtaining credit. The volatility in financial asset values and exchange rates has not caused any structural damage to ASEAN's financial infrastructure. The second wave of tests is likely to start in H2-2009 and continue in the years ahead, even as global and regional economies recover.

What Next?

While the overall impact of the global crisis on ASEAN's financial and banking sectors has been manageable thus far, the region faces some major challenges in the foreseeable future. From a cyclical perspective, ASEAN banks are likely to face a decline in credit quality, which is likely to lead to lower returns as a result of higher write-offs and provisioning. However, we have already caught an early glimpse of international capital flows back into Asia as risk appetite returns, lifting the value of Asian assets. If left unmanaged, this could develop into an asset bubble, which could jeopardize the future stability of the ASEAN financial system.

Structurally, we can expect a major overhaul of the global financial regulatory landscape in the coming years, starting with the developed economies. Financial and banking regulars in the ASEAN region will need to decide whether to cooperate and join the developed world in such reforms or go in their own direction. Cooperation will ensure that the region remains connected and relevant to the global financial and banking system.

Deterioration in Asset Quality

One challenge facing ASEAN banks is a potential decline in credit quality. Weak economic growth and the current liquidity shortage are likely to increase non-performing loans (NPLs). Across ASEAN, there has been a healthy decline in NPLs as a percentage of total loans in recent years (see Table 5.2). Countries such as Malaysia, the Philippines, and Thailand saw their NPL ratios drop from the double digits in 2004–05 to the mid-single digits in 2008. Of course, this was partly the result of rapid lending growth in previous years, which expanded the denominator of the NPL ratio.

TABLE 5.2
Non-performing Loan Ratios (%)

	2003	2004	2005	2006	2007	2008	Latest data
Indonesia	6.8	4.5	7.6	6.1	4.1	3.5	Nov-08
Malaysia	13.9	11.7	9.6	8.5	6.5	5.1	Sep-08
Philippines	16.1	14.4	10.3	7.5	5.8	5.2	Jun-08
Singapore	6.7	5.0	3.8	2.8	1.5	1.4	Sep-08
Thailand	13.5	11.9	9.1	8.4	7.9	6.5	Dec-08

Source: IMF, Global Financial Stability Report, April 2009.

Going forward, NPL ratios are expected to rise given the slowdown in growth and the difficult business environment. The IMF, in its *April 2009 Regional Economic Outlook*, estimated that new writedowns for ASEAN-4 (Indonesia, Malaysia, the Philippines, and Thailand) would be 2.5 per cent of total loans, or 6 per cent including provisions made in 2008. The silver lining is that the ASEAN corporate sector has enjoyed several years of strong growth, which allowed it to reduce leverage and improve profitability and liquidity.

Capital Flows Set to Return to Asia

Looking at private capital flows in and out of the region over the past ten years, one notices that ASEAN has been a consistent net recipient of direct investment flows, averaging US$15 billion per year. 2001 was an exception due to the previous U.S. recession. In terms of portfolio investment, ASEAN saw net annual inflows of between US$5 billion and US$10 billion from 2004–06, followed a marginal outflow in 2007 and a massive outflow of US$57 billion in 2008 as risk aversion surged and foreign investors needed to meet redemption demand from investors back home. In the "other" investment category, which includes trade credit and bank loans, ASEAN has seen outflows in recent years, mainly from Singapore and Malaysia due to their trade activities in the financial sector.

Looking ahead, in 2009 and possibly 2010, direct investment inflows will likely remain subdued due to weak demand from the developed world. China could become a new source of direct

FIGURE 5.8
ASEAN-5[4] Private Capital Flows

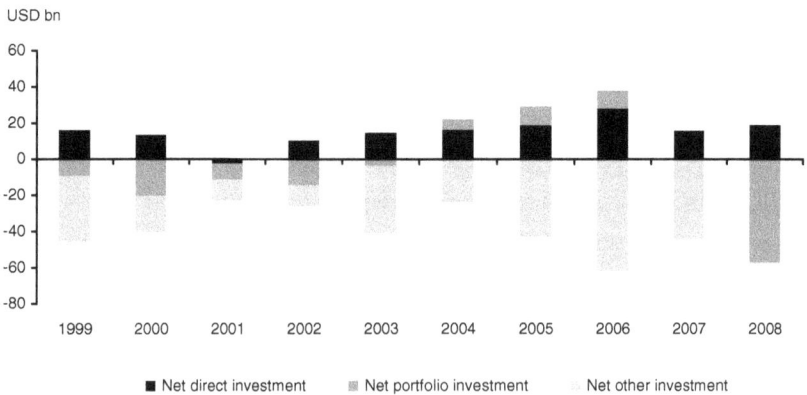

■ Net direct investment   ■ Net portfolio investment   Net other investment

Source: CEIC, SCB Global Research.

investment in the years to come, but is unlikely to be a potent force in the near term. In terms of portfolio investment, there have been some early signs in Q2-2009 that foreign investors are re-entering selected ASEAN markets as risk appetite improves and bargain hunters regain confidence in the region's economic and currency outlook.

Provided that there are further signs of stabilization in the region's economies, portfolio inflows could return to the region in H2-2009 and 2010, though the size and distribution of such flows among regional markets are difficult to predict. There are two areas of concern for authorities. Such capital inflows, alongside current account surpluses in most ASEAN economies, could put upward pressure on Asian currencies, which could prompt intervention by local authorities to limit volatility and curb excessive strength. Furthermore, as we anticipate the recovery in ASEAN economies in 2010 to be modest and subdued, such capital inflows could lift asset valuations above fundamentals. Prevention of asset bubbles should be a key objective of ASEAN central banks as they devise exit strategies from loose monetary policy in the medium term.

The Changing Financial Regulatory Landscape

The financial crisis in the developed world has brought strong demand for regulatory reform of the financial and banking sector. Although the crisis originated in the United States and Europe, such reforms will have global implications. Several areas of reform have been suggested by regulators in the United States, the United Kingdom, and Europe.[5]

1.   **Ensuring adequate capital, both in terms of quantity and quality.** Banks are expected to build up a strong capital

base. It has also been suggested that the level of capital should vary over an economic cycle, being counter-cyclical rather than pro-cyclical. This implies that banks are expected to set aside more capital and prevent excessive lending or balance sheet expansion during times of strong economic growth, and lend more aggressively during economic downturns, to prevent abrupt cutbacks in liquidity.

2. **Further ingraining risk management culture into governance.** There have been calls for banks to adjust their governance structure to increase the independence of risk management functions. Furthermore, the remuneration of bankers should take into account the sustainability of profit and prevent excessive risk-taking behaviour. There are also reviews of whether commercial banks should conduct proprietary trading, which may or may not have direct relevance to their core business.

3. **Extending the reach of regulation across products, financial institutions, and geographies.** There is demand for more oversight of hedge funds and their investment activities in financial markets, including naked short-selling (selling without owning the underlying securities). In the CDS market, it has been suggested that transactions should be centralized and conducted on exchanges rather than being done over the counter. In terms of geography, regulatory bodies are trying extend global financial regulatory agreements to cover offshore financial centres.

4. **Increasing international coordination.** Greater cooperation amongst financial regulators around the world is seen as a must. Exchanging standardized information and data, as well as holding regular discussions on specific issues, should help regulators to better identify potential stress points and learn from the past.

Regulators in the ASEAN region will need to consider the best way to respond to these changes in the regulatory landscape. Given the crucial role of globalization in ASEAN's economic and financial development in the past decade, it would be natural for the region's policy-makers to embrace these changes and be part of the reform process. While there has been strong criticism that inadequate financial supervision and regulation in developed economies led to the current financial crisis, this should not be a reason for ASEAN governments and regulators to ignore global developments. In order to play a more prominent role in the global economy, the region will need to take on-board the regulatory changes being made in the developed world and be ready for them.

In our view, a sensible strategy for the ASEAN region is to adopt a regional framework for banking and financial regulation based on the redesigned global regulatory structure, rather than for each member country to have its own set of rules. This could help to foster the development of banks and financial institutions in the region, as synchronized regulation across the region will reduce regulatory costs for both local and foreign banks. Greater consistency and transparency will also help to attract foreign investors and financial institutions to invest or operate in the region. Meanwhile, by avoiding simply carbon-copying the global standard, the ASEAN financial regulatory framework will provide the flexibility needed to facilitate the development of specific segments or products, especially Islamic banking and financing.

Implications for ASEAN

The global financial crisis has led to considerable volatility in ASEAN financial markets, as well as the region's real economies. While stock market losses were significant and activity in credit and debt markets froze temporarily, the negative impact on foreign exchange, government bonds, and the structural fundamentals of the banking sector has been more manageable. While there are signs of stabilization in the global financial markets and the rate of economic deterioration has slowed, the repercussions for ASEAN's financial and banking sectors are not yet over. Deteriorating credit quality, abrupt capital flows in and out of the region, and an overhaul of the global financial regulatory landscape are some of the challenges these sectors are likely to face in the coming months and years, in the aftermath of the turmoil.

It is also worth noting that the regional markets have been moving in sync. Further to being a reflection of the global liquidity environment, it can also be interpreted that the co-movements of equities and CDS within the region indicate investor perception that the region is becoming more interlinked and interdependent.

This implies that the need for close cooperation and integration within ASEAN is stronger than ever. The protection offered by foreign exchange reserves helps to support investor confidence in times of stress. The bilateral swap lines available to the region under the Chiang Mai Initiative serve this purpose. The proposal to expand this to a multilateral reserve pool of US$120 billion, with contributions from ASEAN, China, Japan, and South Korea, will further strengthen the region's resilience. Even though US$120 billion is a relatively modest amount (less than 5 per cent of Asia's total foreign exchange reserves) at a time when recapitalizing a single financial institution may require tens of billions of dollars, putting the framework in place and agreeing on monitoring and surveillance are key steps forward. Further reserves can be injected into the pool as member countries deem appropriate.

Given the changing global regulatory environment, ASEAN countries may find that prescriptions from the developed world do not perfectly suit local circumstances and conditions. The next best solution in this case would be to have a set of regional standards that build upon the principles of the new financial regulations, which can be seen as adopting global financial regulation, but with ASEAN characteristics. There should be no debate over the principles of adequate capital, independent risk management, more comprehensive regulatory coverage, and international coordination, though how these principles are applied to the region as a whole may be subject to debate. Such a regulatory framework would coincide with ASEAN's strategic goals for the financial services sector, including the promotion of free investment and capital flows, outlined in the ASEAN Economic Community Blueprint.

The global financial crisis has undoubtedly created considerable turbulence in ASEAN's financial and banking sectors, and its impact could linger in the years ahead. Yet the fact that the region has broadly avoided collateral damage to its financial sector should be seen as a positive sign that years of reform and lessons learnt have improved the region's resilience to financial crises. That said, as the global financial landscape continues to evolve and the balance of economic power shifts from the developed economies to emerging markets, the need for improvement continues, and there are opportunities to be captured. We believe further integration within ASEAN is necessary to give the region critical mass amid the rise of China and India, and to ensure that these two powers are partners rather than threats.

Notes

1. This paper was published by the research division of the Standard Chartered Bank, Singapore on 18 June 2009.
2. Association of Southeast Asian Nations (ASEAN) comprises Brunei,

Cambodia, Indonesia, Laos, Malaysia, Myanmar, the Philippines, Singapore, Thailand and Vietnam. Due to data availability, most of the analysis in this paper focus on Indonesia, Malaysia, the Philippines, Singapore, Thailand and Vietnam.

3.	One caveat is that the interbank lending markets in many ASEAN economies are not as mature as in developed economies, and hence interbank market rates may not accurately reflect the level of local-currency liquidity. Moreover, bigger banks, or those with government support, are likely to have better access to interbank liquidity in these markets due to concerns over counterparty risk.

4.	ASEAN-5: Indonesia, Malaysia, the Philippines, Singapore and Thailand.

5.	For more details on the latest thinking, we recommend the *Turner Review*, published by the Financial Services Authority in the United Kingdom.

Hui Cheung Tai is the Regional Head of Research, Southeast Asia in Standard Chartered Bank, Singapore.

6
A BUMPY ROAD TOWARD ASEAN ECONOMIC COMMUNITY 2015

Raymond Atje and Pratiwi Kartika

Introduction

At the ASEAN Summit Meeting in Singapore in November 2007, the ASEAN leaders adopted the ASEAN Economic Community (AEC) Blueprint. AEC is one of the three pillars of the ASEAN Community to be established by 2020. The other two pillars are ASEAN Political and Security Community, and ASEAN Social and Cultural Community. In a declaration which marked the launching of the AEC Blueprint, the ASEAN leaders stated that the AEC "will transform ASEAN into a single market and production base, a highly competitive economic region, a region of equitable economic development, and a region fully integrated into the global economy". AEC is the ultimate goal of ASEAN's deliberate push toward a greater regional economic integration which was started in 1992 when the ASEAN Free Trade Area (AFTA) was launched.[1] There were two other initiatives introduced during the subsequent period, namely, the ASEAN Framework Agreement on Services (AFAS) in 1995, and the ASEAN Investment Area (AIA) in 1998. The three initiatives form the basis for the AEC.

Initially, the full implementation of AEC was scheduled for 2020 but was subsequently moved forward to 2015. The same factors that led to the institutionalization of AEC seem to be behind the decision to expedite its implementation. Firstly, the rapid rise of China not only as a regional but increasingly as a global manufacturing powerhouse. This development raises a concern among ASEAN leaders that, unless the member states agree to deepen and widen the region's economic integration, it will be difficult for ASEAN to compete with China in the global market. It is one reason as why the AEC Blueprint envisions the region as a single production base. Secondly, more recently, India also began to emerge as a regional economic power. Unlike China, India's main strength is in the services sector, most notably the IT sector. In particular, the country's IT sector received a boost from the emergence of global outsourcing mode of production. Finally, there is a concern that ASEAN economies or, more precisely, some member economies seem to get stuck in the so called middle-income trap. On the one hand, their technology is not sophisticated enough to compete with rich countries. On the other hand, their costs of production are not cheap enough to compete with low income countries such as China.[2]

ASEAN as whole has a population of about 575 million, and a combined nominal GDP of US$1282 billion (2007 figures). The idea is, by integrating the region into a single economic entity, it can provide firms operating in the region with economies of scale that will enable them to compete in the global arena. As noted by Pelkmans (2009), the crux of AFTA, and for that matter AEC, is about competitiveness of ASEAN countries in world trade. The idea of a single market and production base is an ambitious one considering that ASEAN is one of the most diverse regions in terms of economic development, culture, and social and political systems. Some of these countries may be regarded as still in the post-colonial stage; they have strong senses of national identity and jealously guard their sovereignties. It may be argued that, because of such a background, ASEAN has opted for a consensus decision-making mechanism, a mechanism that is preserved in the recently adopted ASEAN Charter. Needless to say, such a decision-making process tends to be very slow and the countries involved tend to adhere to the lowest common denominator in every decision to be made.

This paper attempts to assess possible implications of the ongoing global financial crisis on the implementation of AEC, that is, whether the crisis will cause some serious delays in the execution of the roadmap and, hence, in the realization of the AEC by 2015. Almost immediately after the launching of AEC Blueprint, a couple of major external economic shocks began to hit the region one after another and have caused considerable problems to ASEAN member economies. During the first half of 2008, a sharp increase in prices of oil and some other commodities generated inflationary pressure especially in Vietnam where, at one point, the inflation rate reached 25 per cent and banished more people to poverty. This was followed by the current global financial crisis which started in earnest in the second half of the year and already sent Singapore into recession while other member countries saw their economic growth significantly reduced. There is a concern that the current crisis may persuade some ASEAN members to postpone the implementation of the blueprint. Friedman (2005) argues that during a time of economic crisis, people tend to look inward and be less tolerant toward competition from others. It is conceivable therefore that, because of the crisis, some governments in the region may decide to impose protectionist measures so as to placate pressures from certain domestic interest groups.

Unfortunately, under the current circumstances, it is quite difficult for an outsider to monitor and verify such implementation. On the one hand, the ASEAN Secretariat which has been given the task to monitor and review the implementation of the blueprint, may not be able publish the results of its monitoring activities on a timely basis. It simply lacks the capacity to do the job properly. Moreover, rather than collecting all the necessary data and information itself, it relies primarily on relevant government agencies to provide them. On the other hand, the ASEAN Secretariat will disseminate the monitoring results only after being reviewed by senior officials from member states. This limits the effectiveness of the peer pressure mechanism adopted by ASEAN for this purpose. Openness and transparency are essential for a peer pressure mechanism to work. Peer pressure will work effectively if and only if all the reports concerning the implementation of the blueprint are made public in a timely manner.

A Brief Review of AEC

The ASEAN Economic Community Blueprint provides, in the main, important features of the economic community to be established in 2015. Like many other ASEAN documents, the blueprint only outlines the main characteristics of the AEC, leaving the details to further negotiation among the member governments. The first main objective of the blueprint is to establish ASEAN single market and production base. The main characteristics of ASEAN single market and production base are: (i) free flow of goods; (ii) free flow of services; (iii) free flow of investment; (iv) freer flow of capital; and (v) free flow of skilled labour. An ASEAN single market, at least in theory, will generate both tangible and intangible benefits to people of the region. On the one hand, free flow of goods and services within the region, as a manifestation of a single market, will generate welfare gain to people of the region. The deeper and wider the degree of market integration the greater the gain will be.

On the other hand, a larger, single, ASEAN "domestic" market can provide an impetus for industrial agglomeration within the region. There are two channels through which a large market may generate an industrial agglomeration. The first channel is through internal economies scale. Internal economies of scale imply the size of an individual firm matters; larger firms have a costs advantage over smaller ones. In this regards, agglomeration is driven by pecuniary externalities mediated through market prices. A large market allows greater product variety and lower costs (Krugman 1991).[3] The second channel is through external economies of scale, where the size of the industry matters. A firm trying to expand its production will face increasing costs; however, as the industry as a whole expands, the cost of individual firms are lowered.

In view of the foregoing, a large ASEAN market, implied by ASEAN single market, may, in a way, be viewed as a prerequisite for the creation of a single production base in the region. As it is, the idea of a single market as envisioned by the blueprint is quite different from that of the European Union (EU). Free flow of goods simply implies removals of tariff and non-tariff barriers. However, unlike in the EU, shipments of goods from one member country to another will still have to go through border inspection since ASEAN is not a customs union. It should be noted that the removal of tariff and non-tariff barriers are necessary but not sufficient to ensure that a single market will prevail. ASEAN should, in addition, minimize adverse effects of other border and behind border measures through trade facilitation, customs integration, ASEAN single window, harmonization of standards, etc. Finally, for a single market to prevail ASEAN should bring trade costs which include transportation and telecommunication costs down to levels comparable to those in other regions.[4]

With regard to trade in services, the intention is to liberalize all four modes of supply. Yet, the degree of trade liberalization will depend on how officials from the member countries view the notion that "there will be *substantially no restriction* to ASEAN services suppliers in providing services and in establishing companies across national borders within the region, subject to domestic regulations." One should expect tough negotiations ahead since member countries are not allowed to back-load their commitments. Another important issue is the primacy given to domestic regulations in this case. It means a member's commitment to liberalize its trade in services may not contradict the country's domestic regulations pertaining such trade. Finally, while the Minus-X formula may help some members to precede with their liberalization programmes, yet it may also provide other members with a pretext to procrastinate.

Similarly, the notion "free flow of skilled labours" should not be interpreted literally. The movement of skilled labours within the region may not be as free as one would like to think. It is actually managed movements and in addition, mutual recognition arrangement (MR) and certification will still be needed. Conspicuously missing from the blueprint is any attempt to deal with the movement of unskilled labours, while, arguably, it is better if this issue is dealt with at the regional level, since it often involves a number of member countries at the same time. ASEAN should, therefore, have a mechanism to regulate the movement of unskilled labours within the region and the regulation should be as liberal as possible. It seems, however, that the member states are unwilling to do so. They, instead, decide to let this issue to be settled bilaterally between countries involved.

The second important objective of the blueprint is to make ASEAN a competitive economic region. This concept is closely linked to the concept of a single market and production base.

Here a competitive economic region implies that ASEAN-based firms are highly competitive in the global market. In a way, market integration may be viewed as a way to force competitive discipline and efficiency on indigenous companies in ASEAN. But this will happen only if ASEAN domestic markets are highly competitive in the first place.

The third important objective is to eliminate the existing development divide between ASEAN-6, that is, Brunei, Indonesia, Malaysia, the Philippines, Singapore and Thailand on the hand, and Cambodia, Laos, Myanmar and Vietnam (CLMV) on the other. And the last objective is to fully integrate ASEAN into the global economy. To achieve this objective, ASEAN will need substantial amounts of resources. Unfortunately, ASEAN does not have any mechanism to pool its resources, at least not yet. At the moment ASEAN relies mainly on external sources to fund such programmes as the Greater Mekong Sub-region Economic Cooperation Programme clearly illustrates. But it will be difficult for ASEAN to continue relying solely on external sources to finance its Initiative for ASEAN Integration (IAI), or for that matter, its SME development programme. Arguably, it is better for ASEAN if it could somehow mobilize resources of its own to finance, at least partially, its various development projects. In addition to giving ASEAN a sense of ownership of those projects, it will also boost ASEAN's sense of solidarity and unity. Finally, it should also be added that development gaps also exist within some of the ASEAN-6 countries, most notably Indonesia and the Philippines. Arguably, the gaps are comparable in both the degree and magnitude (the number of people involved) to that between ASEAN-6 and CLMV. They too, therefore, require serious attention if ASEAN is to achieve a more equitable community.

ASEAN Economies amid the Global Financial Crisis

Performance of ASEAN Economies

Despite differences in their severity, all countries in Southeast Asia are adversely affected by the global crisis. The most affected economies are Singapore, followed by Thailand and Malaysia, while Indonesia, Vietnam, and the Philippines are less affected. The effects are captured in the region's worsening performance of GDP, investment, trade, and exchange rates since the second semester of 2008. The decline has been more pronounced in Singapore, Malaysia, and Thailand, than others in the region. It seems that the depth of the decline hinges on the sources of their economic growths, with the more affected economies having higher export contribution to growth relative to less affected ones. Singapore has the highest ratio of export to GDP that is, 234 per cent. Since 2006, net export has overtaken investment and consumption to be the key driver of Thailand's economic growth. The increased involvement of the region's countries in the International Production Network has expanded the value of export and, thus, the role of export in boosting the GDP growth. Therefore, the current world crisis which hampers export, inhibited mostly economies with a large dependency on exports.

Table 6.1 illustrates the downward trend of GDP growth. The countries, except the Philippines, started at around the same level of growth in the first quarter 2008. Since then, however, Singapore suffered the most as it rapidly and steadily plunged every quarter and recorded –4 per cent and –10 per cent GDP growths in the last quarter 2008 and first quarter 2009. Thailand has also been hard hit by the crisis since the third quarter 2008 and the economy contracted by 4 per cent and 7 per cent in the

TABLE 6.1

Year-on-Year GDP and Investment Growth of Selected ASEAN Member Countries, 2008–Q1 2009

	Indonesia	Malaysia	Philippines	Singapore	Thailand	Vietnam
Q1-2008 GDP	6.25	7.41	3.92	6.66	5.97	7.52
Investment	13.73	4.59	2.96	30.49	5.44	
Q2-2008 GDP	6.42	6.56	4.16	2.51	5.28	6.54
Investment	12.01	5.62	1.72	24.99	1.94	
Q3-2008 GDP	6.40	4.77	4.56	0.04	3.90	6.52
Investment	12.15	3.06	7.14	14.91	0.64	
Q4-2008 GDP	5.18	0.13	2.85	–4.23	–4.20	6.23
Investment	9.14	–10.22	0.05	–9.92	–3.29	
Q1-2009 GDP	4.37	–6.17	0.45	–10.14	–7.11	3.12
Investment	3.51	–10.83	–5.67	–14.81	–15.79	

Note: Investment refers to Gross Fixed Capital Formation.
Source: CEIC Database.

last quarter 2008 and first quarter 2009. Malaysia also documented similar growth figures with Thailand except for a slightly positive growth of 0.1 per cent in the last quarter 2008. Meanwhile, Indonesia and Vietnam still witnessed robust economic growths of more than 6 per cent during the year 2008. These countries upheld their growth in the first quarter 2009 by growing at 4 per cent and 3 per cent for Indonesia and Vietnam respectively. The Philippines, which historically had lower GDP growth than its neighbours, grew at even slower pace since the last quarter 2008.

Investment in the form of gross fixed capital formation fluctuated in line with the GDP growth. Investment growth of Singapore drastically fell from 30 per cent in the first quarter 2008 to –15 per cent in the same quarter 2009 while that of Indonesia was the most stable among others, declining from 14 per cent in the first quarter 2008 to 3.5 per cent in the last quarter 2009. The size of investment in Malaysia, Thailand, and the Philippines declined significantly at the end of 2008, creating high negative growths in the first quarter 2009.

TABLE 6.2
Year-on-Year Export and Import Growth of Selected ASEAN Member Countries, 2008–April 2009

		Indonesia	Malaysia	Philippines	Singapore	Thailand	Vietnam
Apr, 2008	Export	22.5	20.9	4.9	16.4	16.6	29.1
	Import	106.4	7.9	11.8	26.7	28.6	74.4
May, 2008	Export	31.6	22.9	2.4	12.5	12.5	32.1
	Import	80.7	9.4	11.2	19.0	4.6	73.9
Jun, 2008	Export	34.1	18.6	9.2	10.9	20.6	34.1
	Import	101.3	12.5	13.1	18.7	21.1	34.7
Jul, 2008	Export	24.8	25.3	4.4	15.2	39.7	47.1
	Import	102.3	15.0	16.7	26.8	49.4	39.6
Aug, 2008	Export	29.9	10.7	6.6	7.7	15.2	36.8
	Import	78.2	4.4	1.2	13.7	26.1	20.7
Sep, 2008	Export	29.0	15.0	1.3	11.4	18.2	28.6
	Import	66.3	11.4	3.1	26.2	37.3	8.1
Oct, 2008	Export	4.7	–2.6	–14.4	–4.3	2.4	20.1
	Import	70.7	–5.3	–11.1	4.2	20.9	8.7
Nov, 2008	Export	–1.8	–4.9	–11.4	–11.9	–20.1	–6.3
	Import	16.1	–8.6	–31.5	–9.3	2.5	–19.1
Dec, 2008	Export	–18.7	–14.9	–40.3	–20.4	–11.5	4.3
	Import	13.2	–22.8	–34.0	–16.7	–3.1	–14.3
Jan, 2009	Export	–35.0	–27.8	–40.6	–37.8	–24.6	–25.5
	Import	–31.3	–30.4	–34.5	–33.4	–36.0	–53.8
Feb, 2009	Export	–32.3	–16.0	–39.0	–23.7	–6.6	32.3
	Import	–39.7	–27.6	–31.9	–20.3	–37.1	–27.8
Mar, 2009	Export	–27.9	–15.6	–30.8	–20.7	–16.6	13.0
	Import	–36.2	–28.7	–36.2	–28.1	–29.7	–28.0
Apr, 2009	Export	–22.6	–26.3	n.a.	–26.0	–16.1	–16.1
	Import	–45.2	–22.4	n.a.	–31.1	–27.7	–30.5

Source: CEIC Database.

Exports of all countries in the region have contracted since October 2008. The exception is Vietnam's export which experienced monthly positive growths for a few times since the end of 2008. Indonesia, the Philippines, and Singapore endured the largest proportion of export reduction. Indonesia's export grew by 34 per cent (year-on-year) in January 2008, but fell by about the same percentage in January 2009. The decrease might be due to the end of high commodity-price period. The Philippines' export has also significantly dropped by around 40 per cent per month since December 2008. The reason might be its lack of diversification of export products and destinations since export is highly concentrated in the electronics sector with the United States as its major destination. Falling demand of electronics and declining demand from the United States may have been responsible for the deterioration of the Philippines' export performance. Meanwhile, Singapore's export growth also tumbled to –26 per cent in April 2009.

Import of the Southeast Asian countries fell around 30 per cent in the first quarter 2009. This reflects the weakening domestic purchasing power and less activity of manufacturing industry since the industry usually has high import content.

The global financial crisis has a contagious effect on the countries' local currencies as market confidence in these countries also dropped following the news of recession in the developed economies. Since mid-2008, the Malaysian ringgit, Singaporean dollar, and Thailand baht depreciated after strengthening for quite a long period since 2007. The Vietnamese dong was constant at about VND16,000/USD before continuously weakening from May 2008. The Indonesian rupiah and Filipinos peso were considered to be the more resilient despite an unavoidable depreciation in the last quarter of 2008.

TABLE 6.3

Year-on-Year Inflation of Selected ASEAN Member Countries, 2008–April 2009

	Indonesia	Malaysia	Philippines	Singapore	Thailand	Vietnam
Jan, 2008	6.1	2.3	4.9	6.6	4.3	14.1
Feb, 2008	6.4	2.7	5.4	6.5	5.4	15.7
Mar, 2008	7.1	2.8	6.4	6.7	5.4	19.4
Apr, 2008	7.4	3.0	8.3	7.5	6.1	21.4
May, 2008	8.6	3.8	9.5	7.5	7.6	25.2
Jun, 2008	11.0	7.7	11.4	7.5	8.8	26.8
Jul, 2008	11.9	8.5	12.3	6.5	9.2	27.0
Aug, 2008	11.9	8.5	12.4	6.4	6.5	28.3
Sep, 2008	12.1	8.2	11.8	6.7	6.1	27.9
Oct, 2008	11.8	7.6	11.2	6.4	3.9	26.7
Nov, 2008	11.7	5.7	9.9	5.5	2.2	24.2
Dec, 2008	11.1	4.4	8.0	4.3	0.4	19.9
Jan, 2009	9.2	3.9	7.1	2.9	–0.4	17.5
Feb, 2009	8.6	3.7	7.3	1.9	–0.1	14.8
Mar, 2009	7.9	3.5	6.4	1.6	–0.2	11.3
Apr, 2009	7.3	3.0	4.8	–0.7	–0.9	9.2

Source: CEIC Database.

Unlike other indicators, inflation showed improvement since mid-2008. Prices have been more stable, with Thailand and Singapore recording year-on-year deflation in April 2009. Vietnam had the most volatile prices, reaching an inflation rate of 28 per cent in August 2008 before dropping to 9 per cent in April 2009. The contributing factor of this price control may be the falling of oil and commodity prices.

Policy Responses to the Crisis

Governments took policy actions as their response to the crisis in order to minimize its adverse impact and boost economic growth.

Governments in the region generally eased monetary policy and injected fiscal stimulus. Liquidity problem arose and, therefore, certain policy actions were taken to overcome this. Singapore ensured the liquidity of its Singapore dollar by monetary operations and standing facility. To enhance the flow of credit to the real sector, Singapore also initiated the Special Risk-sharing Initiative (SRI), that is, a government programme to cover 75 per cent of risk borne by banks providing working capital and trade financing loans to businesses. Other countries in the region loosened their monetary stance later than those in East Asia. Indonesia and the Philippines were struggling with high inflationary pressure in 2008 due to oil and commodity price hikes. Interest rates remained high until December 2008, when they started to gradually trim the benchmark interest rates. This interest rate downward rigidity was probably the reason behind the liquidity problem in the banking sector. To increase liquidity, central banks cut the bank's statutory reserve requirement. Thailand has also lessened its key interest rate from 3.75 per cent to 2 per cent although the central bank has acknowledged the limited effectiveness of Thailand's monetary transmission to the real sector via interest rates.

Fiscal stimulus packages were introduced to domestic economies, mostly taking the forms of infrastructure projects and tax cuts. Indonesia disbursed Rp 78 trillion (US$7.8 billion); around 60 per cent of which are to cover income tax reduction. The rest is for subsidy and government expenditure such as infrastructure project and rural sector development. Thailand implemented a stimulus package of THB117 billion (US$3.4 billion), THB19 billion of which has been distributed as cash handouts to low-income people. The rest will be spent on education, public works in rural areas, transportation and utility provision, and financial assistance to enterprises. The Philippines planned to stimulate the economy with PHP330 billion (US$6.8 billion) in 2009, mostly for infrastructure projects. Malaysia had also realized its first stimulus package of RM7 billion (US$2 billion) in November 2008 although there are doubts on the effectiveness of the package. Another package of RM15 billion will also be disbursed in 2009. Singapore stimulated its economy by introducing the Job Credit Scheme, that is, cash granted to enterprises for them to keep hiring the employees.

Possible Implications of the Current Crisis on Achieving AEC Goals

There are a number of reasons why some countries may want to delay the implementation of the AEC Blueprint. First, governments are under intense domestic pressure to stop or even reverse economic reforms, especially trade liberalization. As suggested by Friedman (2005), such pressure tends to intensify during a time of crisis. And as the foregoing discussion clearly shows, ASEAN countries are experiencing adverse effects of the current global financial crisis, albeit with different degrees of severity. Second, quite often economic reforms lead to reallocation of resources from one group of people to another and therefore, tend to generate winners and losers, at least in the short run. It is one reason as to why economic reforms often encounter oppositions from those who are likely to be losers. Finally, member governments do not consider the implementation of the blueprint as their top priority or are even under an impression that the blueprint is not binding.

Some governments may therefore be tempted to use the current crisis as an excuse to defer the implementation of the blueprint. However, it is worth noting that, despite the crisis, no ASEAN country has openly declared its intention to defer the implementation of the blueprint. Moreover, it may be argued that a deferment is likely to have only a marginal impact, if at all, on the economic performance of the country. The reason is because ASEAN countries trade primarily with non-ASEAN countries, hence the removing of all barriers to intra-ASEAN trade is unlikely to worsen their trade performance. In addition, the implementation of the blueprint is done in an incremental way. Yet, the damage of a deferment to the regional cooperation is likely to be long-lasting. It will certainly damage the reputation not only of the country involved but also of ASEAN as whole.

Nevertheless, the fact that no member has stated its intention to defer the implementation of the blueprint does not necessarily mean that it will actually be implemented as scheduled. Alas, as noted earlier, it is not always easy for outsiders to find out the status of implementation of the blueprint for two reasons. First, the ASEAN Secretariat tasked to monitor the implementation of the blueprint does not have the capacity to do the job properly. They have many other duties beside this one. In addition, the ASEAN Secretariat depends primarily on inputs of government agencies of the member states. It may serve these agencies' own interests not to reveal the actual status of the blueprint implementation.

Second, even if the ASEAN Secretariat is able to detect any infringement of the blueprint objectives on time, it may not be able to release the findings to the general public. On the one hand, as with many other ASEAN documents, a report concerning the implementation of the blueprint has to be reviewed by senior government officials from the member states before the ASEAN Secretariat can disclose it to the public. They (the officials) can stop the disclosure if they deem the report will hurt their countries' interests. It is possible, therefore, that the ASEAN Secretariat will not publish the report or publish a watered-down version of it.

On the other hand, to make sure that the members will implement the blueprint, ASEAN is relying purely on a peer pressure mechanism devoid of any notion of adversarial approach to dispute resolution among members. In addition, ASEAN also shuns the use of penalties against those who evade their obligations under the blueprint. All of these, coupled with the existing monitoring mechanism, will certainly limit the effectiveness of the ASEAN Secretariat's monitoring mechanism and the peer pressure that comes with it. The peer pressure mechanism will work effectively only if the monitoring report is published as it is and on a timely basis. In addition members should be able to convey their dissatisfaction with, and put pressure on, other members that fail to implement the blueprint.

One way to temporarily mitigate this problem is to encourage all stakeholders, particularly the business community and news media, to participate in monitoring of the implementation of blueprint and publish their findings. In the long run, ASEAN should establish an independent monitoring body to monitor the development towards the AEC in particular, and the ASEAN Community in general.

The foregoing discussion clearly indicates that the success or failure of ASEAN to establish the ASEAN Economic Community by 2015 depends primarily on the commitments of the member states to implement the blueprint. Understandably, ASEAN countries' attention may have been distracted by the current global financial crisis but they should not be paralyzed by it. Open economies like those of ASEAN are bound to experience economic shocks, external or otherwise, from time to time. But, as argued above, they should not use the crisis as a pretext to delay the implementation of the blueprint.

Conclusion

This paper argues that the road toward AEC 2015 is bumpy. Firstly, some member governments may not see the implementation of the blueprint as their top priority. Some implementing bodies may not even consider the blueprint as binding. The current crisis may push the implementation of the blueprint further down in their priority lists. Secondly, ASEAN members are among the most open economies in the world. As it is, they are susceptible external economic shocks such as the current global financial crisis. In other words, the region is likely to experience economic shocks from time to time which may divert the members' attention from implementing the blueprint as scheduled.

To mitigate this problem, ASEAN should improve its monitoring mechanism to enable it to detect non-compliance as early as possible and to publish its finding on a regular basis and as transparently as possible. Arguably, it is better if such as task is done by an independent body. In addition, ASEAN should remind its members that the implementation of blueprint is a binding commitment.

Another issue that needs further attention is how to treat the losers. As noted earlier, economic reforms, especially those that involve reallocation of resources tend to generate winners and losers, at least in the short run. ASEAN should find a way to dampen opposition from the likely losers. ASEAN should at least ensure its members that this problem is not their problem alone but also of ASEAN as an institution.

Notes

1. There had been a number of other regional economic cooperation initiatives introduced prior to 1992 such as the ASEAN Industrial Project (AIP), the ASEAN Preferential Trading Arrangement (PTA), ASEAN Industrial Joint Venture (AIJV), and ASEAN Industrial Cooperation (AICO). All these initiatives ended up in failure, however.

2.   According to Eeckhout and Jovanovic (2007), the middle income
      trap phenomenon is a consequence of international mobility of
      labour service made possible by global outsourcing. In their model,
      rich countries specialize in design and managerial work, while
      poor countries specialize in wage work.

3.   ASEAN firms will be able to take advantage of a larger ASEAN
      market only if each member country treats firms of other members
      as equal, in every respect, to its own firms. In other words, ASEAN
      members should apply national treatment to each other firms, not
      just with regard to investment, but in every other aspect that matters
      to firms' expansion.

4.   Even if all of these have been achieved, the ASEAN market that is
      emerging may remain fragmented. Moreover, there is no guarantee
      that a single production base will emerge either. A number of
      empirical studies on U.S.-Canada cross border trades show that
      borders matter a lot even after the existing trade barriers have
      been substantially removed. A study by McCallum (1995) for
      instance show that, other things being equal, Canadian firms trade
      far more with each other than with U.S. companies. Similar findings
      for the EU have been reported as well (for example, see Head and
      Mayer 2000). In addition, a single production base is more likely to
      emerge if ASEAN intra-regional trade costs fall below a certain
      threshold level.

References

Eeckhout, Jan and Boyan Jovanovic. "Occupational Choice and
      Development". NBER Working Paper No. 13686, 2007.
Friedman, Benjamin M. *The Moral Consequence of Economic Growth*.
      New York: Vintage Books, 2005.
Head, Keith and Thierry Mayer. "Non-Europe: The Magnitude and Causes
      of Market Fragmentation in the EU". *Weltwirtschaftliches Archiv*
      136, no. 2 (2000): 285–314.

Krugman, Paul. "Increasing Returns and Economic Geography". *Journal of Political Economy* 99 (1991): 483–99.

McCallum, John. "National Borders Matter: Canada-U.S. Regional Trade Patterns". *American Economic Review* 85 (1995): 615–23.

Pelkmans, Jacques. "The ASEAN Economic Community: Dilemma's of a Shallow Trading Club". UNU-CRIS Working Paper W-2009/5, 2009.

Raymond Atje is the head of the Department of Economics at the Centre for Strategic and International Studies (CSIS), Jakarta.

Pratiwi Kartika is a research staff at the Department of Economics at the Centre for Strategic and International Studies (CSIS), Jakarta.

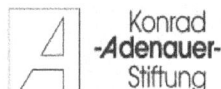

ASEAN ROUNDTABLE 2009
THE GLOBAL ECONOMIC CRISIS:
IMPLICATIONS FOR ASEAN

Thursday, 18 June 2009
Pan Pacific Hotel, Singapore

PROGRAMME

Wednesday, 17 June 2009

7.00 p.m.   Welcome Dinner for Speakers, Discussants and
                        Chairpersons
                        Global Kitchen Café, Pan Pacific Hotel

Thursday, 18 June 2009

8.30 a.m. – 9.00 a.m.   Registration

9.00 a.m. – 9.15 a.m.   **OPENING REMARKS**

                        Ambassador K. KESAVAPANY
                        Director, Institute of Southeast Asian Studies,
                        Singapore

                        Dr Colin DUERKOP
                        Regional Representative for Southeast Asia,
                        Konrad Adenauer Stiftung,
                        Singapore

	SESSION I	**STRATEGIC AND POLITICAL IMPLICATIONS**
	Chairperson	*Dr CHIN Kin Wah* Deputy Director, Institute of Southeast Asian Studies, Singapore
9.15 a.m. – 10.15 a.m.	**Paper 1:**	**How will the Crisis Affect the Realization of the ASEAN Political and Security Community?**
	Paperwriter:	*Professor Herman Joseph S. KRAFT* Assistant Professor, Department of Political Science, University of the Philippines-Diliman
	Discussant:	*Dr Natasha HAMILTON-HART* Associate Professor, Southeast Asian Studies, National University of Singapore
10.15 a.m. – 11.00 a.m.	**Paper 2:**	**Will Changes in Economic Relationships have an Impact on Existing Strategic Relationships (within ASEAN and with Dialogue Partners)?**
	Paperwriter:	*Dr YEO Lay Hwee* Director, European Union Centre, Singapore
	Discussion	
11.00 a.m. – 11.15 a.m.	**Coffee**	

SESSION II THE SOCIAL CONSEQUENCES

Chairperson: *Mr Rodolfo SEVERINO*
Head, ASEAN Studies Centre,
Institute of Southeast Asian Studies,
Singapore

11.15 a.m. – 12.00 noon **Paper 3:** **ASEAN's Response Mechanisms for Labour and Social Protection: Challenges in Creating Crisis-Resilient Economies**

Presenter: *Mr Peter VAN ROOIJ*
Deputy Director,
International Labour Organisation,
Jakarta and ASEAN Liaison,
Indonesia

12.00 noon – 1.00 p.m. **Paper 4:** **What Can ASEAN do to Address Rising Poverty Levels and Social Unrest?**

Paperwriter: *Professor LIM Teck Ghee*
Professorial Fellow,
Malaysian Institute of Development
and Asian Studies, UCSI University,
Malaysia

Discussion

1.00 p.m. – 2.30 p.m. **Lunch**

Distinguished Luncheon Speaker
Mr Arin JIRA
Chairman
ASEAN Business Advisory Council

Presentation of Gift of ISEAS Books to Myanmar Libraries

To be presented by ISEAS Director Ambassador Kesavapany to H.E. Win Myint, Myanmar Ambassador to Singapore

**SESSION III IMPACT ON ECONOMY AND
FINANCE**

Chairperson: *Dr Omkar Lal SHRESTHA*
              Visiting Senior Research Fellow,
              Institute of Southeast Asian Studies,
              Singapore

2.30 p.m. – 3.15 p.m.   **Paper 5:**   **How is ASEAN Coping with the
                                         Economic Vulnerabilities that have
                                         Emerged from the Crisis?**

                         Presenter: *Mr LIM Chze Cheen*
                                         Assistant Director of Strategic
                                         Planning and Coordination Division,
                                         ASEAN Secretariat,
                                         Indonesia

                         Discussant: *Emeritus Professor Datuk Dr
                                         Mohamed ARIFF*
                                         Executive Director,
                                         Malaysian Institute of Economic
                                         Research (MIER),
                                         Malaysia

3.15 p.m. – 4.30 p.m.   **Paper 6:**   **How are the Financial and Banking
                                         Sectors in ASEAN Faring and
                                         Coping?**

                         Paperwriter: *Mr HUI Cheung Tai*
                                         Regional Head of Research,
                                         South East Asia,
                                         Standard Chartered Bank,
                                         Singapore

                         Discussant: *Mr Jaseem AHMED*
                                         Director, Southeast Asia Department,
                                         Asian Development Bank

4.30 p.m. – 5.15 p.m.   **Paper 7:**   **What Would be the Implications of This Crisis on Building an ASEAN Economic Community by 2015?**

Paperwriter: *Dr Raymond ATJE*
Head, Economics,
Centre for Strategic and International Studies,
Jakarta

Discussion

5.15 p.m. – 5.30 p.m.   **Closing Remarks**

Mr Rodolfo SEVERINO
Head, ASEAN Studies Centre,
Institute of Southeast Asian Studies,
Singapore

Dr Wilhelm HOFMEISTER
Regional Representative for Southeast Asia,
Konrad Adenauer Stiftung,
Singapore

5.30 p.m.   **TEA RECEPTION**
(Farewell to Dr Colin Duerkop and welcome to Dr Wilhelm Hofmeister)

ANNEX II

ASEAN ROUNDTABLE 2009
THE GLOBAL ECONOMIC CRISIS:
IMPLICATIONS FOR ASEAN

Thursday, 18 June 2009
Pacific Ballrooms I & II
Pan Pacific Hotel, Singapore

LIST OF PARTICIPANTS

Chairpersons and Presenters

1. Mr Jaseem AHMED
    Director
    Asian Development Bank
    Southeast Asia Department
    6 ADB Avenue, Mandaluyong City
    Metro Manila
    Philippines
    Tel: (632) 6326 455
    Fax: (632) 6362 331
    Email: jahmed@adb.org

2. Dr Mohamed ARIFF
    Executive Director
    The Malaysian Institute of Economic Research
    Level 2, Podium, City Point
    Kompleks Dayabumi
    Jalan Sultan Hishamuddin
    P O Box 12160
    50768 Kuala Lumpur
    Malaysia
    Tel: (603) 2272 5897
    Fax: (603) 2273 0197
    Email: ariff@mier.po.my

3.   Dr Raymond ATJE
      Head, Department of Economics
      Centre for Strategic and International Studies
      The Jakarta Post Building, 3rd Fl.
      Jalan Palmerah Barat NO. 142-143,
      Jakarta 10270
      Indonesia
      Tel: (6221) 5365 4601
      Fax: (6221) 5365 4607
      Email: raymond_atje@csis.or.id

4.   Dr CHIN Kin Wah
      Deputy Director
      Institute of Southeast Asian Studies
      30 Heng Mui Keng Terrace
      Pasir Panjang
      Singapore 119614
      Tel: (65) 6870 2433
      Fax: (65) 6778 1735
      Email: chinkw@iseas.edu.sg

5.   Ms Sanchita Basu DAS
      Visiting Research Fellow, ASEAN Studies Centre
      Institute of Southeast Asian Studies   ·
      30 Heng Mui Keng Terrace
      Pasir Panjang
      Singapore 119614
      Tel: (65) 6870 4511
      Fax: (65) 6775 6264
      Email: sanchita@iseas.edu.sg

6.   Dr Colin DUERKOP
      Regional Representative for Southeast Asia
      Konrad Adenauer Stiftung Singapore
      34 Bukit Pasoh Road
      Singapore
      Tel: (65) 6227 2001
      Fax: (65) 6227 8342
      Email: duerkop@kas-asia.org

7.   Dr Natasha HAMILTON-HART
        Associate Professor
        National University of Singapore
        Southeast Asian Studies
        AS3, Art Link
        Singapore 117570
        Tel: (65) 6516 7934
        Fax: (65) 6777 6608
        Email: seahhne@nus.edu.sg

8.   Dr Wilhelm HOFMEISTER
        Regional Representative for Southeast Asia
        Konrad Adenauer Stiftung Singapore
        34 Bukit Pasoh Road
        Singapore
        Tel: (65) 6227 2001
        Fax: (65) 6227 8343
        Email: wilhelm.hofmeister@kas.de

9.   Mr HUI Cheung Tai
        Regional Head of Research, SE Asia
        Global Research
        Standard Chartered Bank Singapore
        6 Battery Road, #03-00,
        Singapore 049909
        Tel: (65) 6530 3464
        Fax: (65) 6789 3756
        Email: tai.hui@sc.com

10.   Mr Arin JIRA
        Chairman
        ASEAN Business Advisory Council
        c/o ASEAN-BAC Secretariat
        70 A, Jl. Sisingamangaraja, Jakarta 12110
        Indonesia
        Tel: (6221) 722 0705
        Fax: (6221) 722 0539
        Email: arinj@bigth.com

11.   Ambassador K. KESAVAPANY
      Director
      Institute of Southeast Asian Studies
      30 Heng Mui Keng Terrace
      Pasir Panjang
      Singapore 119614
      Tel: (65) 6778 0955
      Fax: (65) 6778 1735
      Email: kesavapany@iseas.edu.sg

12.   Mr Herman Joseph KRAFT
      Assistant Professor
      University of the Philippines-Diliman
      Department of Political Science
      Diliman, Quezon City, The Philippines
      Tel: (632) 981 8500
      Fax: (632) 920 7246
      Email: hkraft@kssp.edu.upd.ph / herman_joseph.kraft@up.edu.ph

13.   Mr LIM Chze Cheen
      Assistant Director of Strategic Planning and Coordination Division
      ASEAN Secretariat Jakarta
      70A Jalan Sisingamangaraja
      Tel: (6221) 726 2991 (Ext. 310)
      Fax: (6221) 739 8234
      Email: Cheen@asean.org

14.   Professor LIM Teck Ghee
      Professorial Fellow
      Malaysian Institute of Development and Asian Studies
      UCSI University
      UCSI North Wing Campus, Jalan Choo Lip Kung,
      Taman Taynton View, Cheras,
      Kuala Lumpur 56000
      Malaysia
      Tel: (603) 9101 8880
      Fax: (603) 2278 8033
      Email: tglim1@gmail.com

15.   Mr Peter Van ROOIJ
       Deputy Director of ILO Jakarta Office
       International Labour Organization
       ILO Jakarta Office, Menara Thamrin Level 22,
       Jalan MH Thamrin Kav. 3
       Jakarta 10250
       Indonesia
       Tel: (6221) 391 3112
       Fax: (6221) 310 0766
       Email: vanrooij@ilo.org

16.   Mr Rodolfo SEVERINO
       Head, ASEAN Studies Centre
       Institute of Southeast Asian Studies
       30 Heng Mui Keng Terrace
       Pasir Panjang
       Singapore 119614
       Tel: (65) 6870 4524
       Fax: (65) 6775 6264
       Email: severino@iseas.edu.sg

17.   Dr Omkar Lal SHRESTHA
       Visiting Senior Research Fellow
       Institute of Southeast Asian Studies
       30 Heng Mui Keng Terrace
       Pasir Panjang
       Singapore 119614
       Tel: (65) 6870 4531
       Fax: (65) 6775 6264
       Email: oshrestha@iseas.edu.sg

18.   Ms Moe THUZAR
       Visiting Research Fellow, ASEAN Studies Centre
       Institute of Southeast Asian Studies
       30 Heng Mui Keng Terrace
       Pasir Panjang
       Singapore 119614
       Tel: (65) 6870 4512
       Fax: (65) 6775 6264
       Email: moe@iseas.edu.sg

19.   Dr YEO Lay Hwee
        Director
        European Union Centre
        National University of Singapore / Nanyang Technology University
        11 Slim Barracks Rise, #06-01
        Executive Centre, NTU@one-north campus
        Singapore 138664
        Tel: (65) 6513 2006
        Fax: (65) 6774 1445
        Email: eucylh@nus.edu.sg / ylh@pacific.net.sg

ISEAS

20.   Dr Pavin Chachavalpongpun
        Visiting Research Fellow, ASEAN Studies Centre
        Institute of Southeast Asian Studies
        30 Heng Mui Keng Terrace
        Pasir Panjang
        Singapore 119614
        Tel: (65) 6870 4522
        Fax: (65) 6775 6264
        Email: pavin@iseas.edu.sg

21.   Mr Deepak NAIR
        Research Associate
        Institute of Southeast Asian Studies
        Email: deepak@iseas.edu.sg

21.   Mr Mark TALLARA
        Research Assistant, ASEAN Studies Centre
        Institute of Southeast Asian Studies
        Email: mtallara@iseas.edu.sg

22.   Mr Kenneth TAN
        Institute of Southeast Asian Studies